The
ATTITUDE
IS
EVERYTHING
Workbook

ALSO BY KEITH HARRELL

Attitude Is Everything

The
ATTITUDE
—— IS ——
EVERYTHING
Workbook

Strategies and Tools for Developing

Personal and Professional Success

KEITH HARRELL

 HarperBusiness

An Imprint of HarperCollinsPublishers

HarperCollins books may be purchased for educational, business, or sales promotional use. For information please write: Special Markets Department, HarperCollins Publishers Inc., 10 East 53rd Street, New York, New York 10022.

Designed by William Ruoto

Library of Congress Cataloging-in-Publication Data has been applied for.

ISBN 0060507136

03   04   05   06   07   RRD   10   9   8   7   6   5   4   3   2   1

This workbook is dedicated with the greatest love

and affection to my family and friends for their love,

support, and encouragement. And most important,

to God for giving me everything—life, knowledge,

wisdom, and the ability to do his work.

ACKNOWLEDGMENTS

I would like to thank my trusted friend and communication consultant W. Scott Holloway for his invaluable counsel, commitment, and dedication. You have faithfully and selflessly given of your time and energy on this project to help make the concept of this workbook a reality.

In addition, thanks to the support team of Jan Miller and HarperCollins for their commitment in getting this worthwhile project completed.

A special thanks goes out to all of you who have purchased this book and are beginning the journey toward self-empowerment. I honor your courage, your commitment, and your dedication.

CONTENTS

INTRODUCTION

"Attitude Is Everything!" It's important to recognize the need to manage and control the quality of your life through the power of a positive attitude. Attitude is the foundation and support of everything we do, a key element in the process of controlling your destiny and achieving mastery in your personal and professional life.

If you want a positive attitude, your're going to need to be committed enough to work at it. This workbook is a guide toward developing an attitude that will work for you rather than against you. I will provide you with the information and the plan. It's up to you to provide the effort and discipline to put the plan into action. It will take some work on your part, but I promise you will get a wonderful return on your investment.

Over the years, I've attended countless seminars, read hundreds of books, listened to hours and hours of tapes, and interviewed scores of successful people on the subject of self-development. I've discovered that learning to monitor, control, and tap into a positive attitude is the key to every self-help process. In fact, *the most valuable asset you can possess is a positive attitude toward your life.* Although the process I've mapped out is not always easy, I have broken the information down into manageable parts to make your goals easier to reach.

The underlying principle of this entire workbook is simple. I believe that by changing your thinking, you can change your beliefs. I further believe that by changing your beliefs, you can change your actions. And finally I believe that by changing your actions, you can change your life. The hard part is going to be putting this principle into action.

It is my objective in this workbook to help you to triumph over life's challenges and empower you to seize control over your life.

I encourage you to use this workbook in conjunction with *Attitude Is Everything* CDs, audio and video cassettes, and books, or you can use it as a stand-alone guide toward the attainment of a healthy and positive attitude.

We have given this workbook special attention to ensure that it has what it takes to help you achieve maximum results. We ask that you give this course your special attention that you may get the maximum results possible and produce positive results in your life.

Remember, *the most valuable asset you can possess is a positive attitude toward life!*

Enjoy the workbook and have a super-fantastic life,

Keith Harrell

THE
ATTITUDE
IS
EVERYTHING
WORKBOOK

STEP I

"UNDERSTAND THE POWER OF ATTITUDE"

How we think shows through in how we act.
Attitudes are mirrors of the mind.
They reflect our thinking.

—David Joseph Schwartz

**TTITUDE PLAYS AN** important role in everyone's life. Many people don't know its meaning or realize the influence attitude has on the quality of their life experience. Your attitude influences your entire personal and professional life. What we think about the most influences how we feel. What we think about influences our attitude. We are consistently moving in the direction of our most dominant thoughts. If our dominant thoughts are healthy and positive they result in a healthy and positive attitude. If our dominant thoughts are unhealthy and negative they result in an unhealthy and negative attitude.

So, what is attitude and how does attitude impact life? The *American Heritage Dictionary* defines attitude as a state of mind or feeling with regard to some matter. For me, attitude can be defined in one word: *life.* Your attitude dictates whether you are living life or life is living you. Attitude determines whether you are on the way or in the way. Attitude is your perception of life, which is either a failure-reinforcing perspective or a success-reinforcing perspective. Attitude is the means by which you come to arrive at a level of performance, in all that you do, that is either constructive or destructive. The attitude that you carry around makes an incredible difference in your life. It can be a powerful tool for positive action—or it can be a poison that cripples your ability to fulfill your potential. Attitude is life! Just as every living human being has life, every living human being has attitude. Just as every human has unique attributes about his or her life, so does every human have unique attributes about his or her attitude. Everyone has attitude; however, you and I both know, everyone does not have the same attitude.

How many times have we all had the experience of greeting a stranger, co-worker, store clerk, waiter/waitress, friend, or relative and in one instance the person was warm, pleasant, and reciprocating and in another instance we have greeted the same or yet another stranger, co-worker, store clerk, waiter/waitress, friend, or relative who was cold and unfriendly? What was the difference? Was it simply a matter of circumstance? The unadulterated and irrefutable truth is that the difference was in their attitude!

George Bernard Shaw said, "People are always blaming their circumstances for what they are. . . . The people who get on in this world are the people who get up and look for the circumstances they want and, if they can't find them, make them." How do we make the circumstances we want when we, in most instances, do not choose our circumstances? The answer to this question is that our control is not found in our choosing circumstances; it is found in our response to the circumstances we experience! This is the difference between living internally and living externally. People with a positive attitude are influenced by what goes on within them. People with a negative attitude are influenced by what goes on around them. We improve our circumstances by improving our responses to them. Our improved responses are adequate enough to improve our circumstances.

Optimists (individuals with positive attitudes) are more successful than similarly talented people with pessimistic or negative attitudes, according to Martin Seligman, a noted psychologist at the University of Pennsylvania. His research also indicates that negative attitudes can be changed to positive attitudes. Seligman's study has shown that our attitudes—positive or negative—can affect whether we succeed or fail in reaching our goals. In his classic book, *Learned Optimism,* he offers empirical data showing that life insurance agents with optimistic attitudes sold more policies than did their pessimistic colleagues. Pessimists blamed failed sales attempts on themselves, which lowered their self-esteem and led to lower sales volumes. Optimists, rather than taking the rejections personally, had logical reasons to explain why prospects did not buy policies. Optimists not only sold 37 percent more policies than their pessimistic colleagues, they also remained on the job longer.

Notice the difference between the two groups. The optimists rationally and logically searched for and discovered specific remedies to their challenge. They tried new things and through the process of elimination discovered what works for them. The pessimists, on the other hand, deduced without careful reasoning that they were the reason for their poor performance. They continued to do the same old things the same old way, expecting a different outcome, and it eventually deteriorated their self-esteem to the degree that most quit their jobs. The differences in the manner in which the optimists and the pessimists dealt with their challenges are significant!

The power of positive thinking has been documented scientifically. There are proven rewards in your choosing to develop a process for developing and maintaining a positive attitude. Each of us can decide to change our negative attitude or improve upon our positive attitude. Most people get health or dental checkups once or twice a year to maintain wellness. We take our cars to mechanics to make sure they keep running properly. Yet, sadly, we aren't nearly as careful about monitoring the attitudes that affect every aspect of our lives. When was the last time you had an attitude checkup? If you haven't been getting what you want out of life, if people are not responding well to you, could it be that you need one? At Harrell Performance Systems Incorporated we offer a series of products and services that are complementary to this workbook. Each "Attitude" product and/or service is specially designed to give you, your family, or your organization the important attitude tune-up skills needed for lifelong success. Call us at (770) 451-3190 to receive a list of the products and services available to you. Also visit our website at www.superfantastic.com.

I spent most of my young adulthood chasing a dream to become a professional basketball player. In high school, I was an All-American and the Most

Valuable Player of our state championship team. I accepted a scholarship to Seat-tle University, where I was the team captain for three of my four years. I averaged more than sixteen points per game in my senior year. In June 1979 I expected to be drafted by a National Basketball Association team. It was the dream that I had shared with everyone I knew. My family, friends, teammates, and others who had followed my career had come to expect that it would happen, based on my success as a player in high school and college. I had no reason to think otherwise.

On the day of the NBA draft, I waited and waited and waited . . . but the phone did not ring. I was devastated. I had devoted myself to the sport and to my future as an NBA player. It was tough to give up on that dream. I felt cheated when it didn't happen.

In the days and weeks that followed, the bitterness was revived every time someone commented on my failure to be drafted. It didn't help when strangers would note my six-foot-six-inch height and say, "You must play pro basketball." For a long time I fought the bitterness. Finally I decided to let go of the negative feelings. I found a way to embrace this major change and focus on being positive instead. I realized that to grow inwardly I had to move on with my life. I gave myself an attitude checkup and realized I wasn't getting out of life what I desired. I realized that people were not responding to me well because I was not respond-ing well toward them. I developed a new and positive attitude. Shortly thereafter, while I was attending a luncheon, a woman seated next to me asked if I played with the NBA. "Yes I do," I replied. "I'm a first-round draft choice. I'm the most valuable player. I'm owner of the team, and we win the championship every year!"

"So you do play with the NBA?" she asked.

"Yes, I do. I play with my *Natural Born Abilities*, and I'm slam-dunking every day!" I could have held on to my negative attitude. I could have been rude and obnoxious to this lady who did not deserve it. Instead I chose to work to develop and work to maintain a healthy, positive attitude—and with your help, I am going to teach you to do the same using the techniques outlined in this workbook.

YOUR ATTITUDE REFLECTS YOU

Although everyone has an attitude, not everyone has the same type of attitude. Some individuals have optimistic attitudes that propel them along, helping them deal with challenges, overcome obstacles, and accomplish their objectives.

The following are examples of an optimist:

No matter what happens, Ann always has a smile on her face.
Carl always manages to find the good in even the worst of situations.
Lisa can get anything done. She is assertive and unstoppable.
Jim is an inspiration. He has empathy while maintaining a results-oriented focus.

Others have attitudes that are anchors, slowing them down or stopping them altogether, interfering with their ability to live up to their full potential. The following are examples of a pessimist:

Bob is not a devil's advocate. He's just plain negative.
Sue's focus is always on the problem. She should try to focus on the solution.
Larry never has good things to say about his job. Why doesn't he get a new job?
If I don't get the promotion and Becky does, I will quit!

Think of *everyone* you know personally and identify each person by his or her attitude. List the attributes of their optimism or their pessimism. Use codes or fake names to identify the people you know. Follow the examples above.

Optimists:

_____

_____

_____

_____

_____

_____

_____

_____

_____

_____

_____

_____

_____

_____

_____

_____

_____

_____

Pessimists:

_____

_____

_____

_____

_____

_____

_____

_____

_____

_____

_____

_____

_____

_____

_____

_____

_____

_____

Each of us has experienced a situation where we see someone coming toward us and we frown and say to ourselves, "Here he comes again!" Each of us has also experienced a situation where we smile and say to ourselves, "I cannot wait until he comes again!" The difference between these two responses is that the first person has developed a reputation for exasperating us in some way, while person number two has developed a reputation for gratifying us in some way.

Because we gravitate toward positive people if we are positive, when negative people come around us they exasperate us. Only other positive people can gratify a positive person. Because we gravitate toward negative people if we are negative, when positive people come around us they exasperate us. Only other negative people can gratify a negative person. "Birds of a feather flock together!"

What type of reputation would you say you have with others?

Positive _____   Negative _____

Would you identify yourself as an optimist or a pessimist?

Optimist _____   Pessimist _____

When faced with challenges and difficulties, do you focus on staying positive or do you give in to the pressure of negative circumstances?

Positive _____   Negative _____

Do you help to eliminate challenges and difficulties or do you contribute to challenges and difficulty?

Eliminate _____   Contribute _____

When you identified everyone you knew personally and identified them as optimists or pessimists, which of the two lists was easier to write?

Optimists _____   Pessimists _____

When you identified everyone you knew personally and identified them as optimists or pessimists, which list had the most names?

Optimists _____   Pessimists _____

Whichever list was the easier of the two to prepare, or the longer, serves as a representation of your attitude. If your list of optimists was the easier to write and is your longer list, this workbook will help you to fine-tune your attitude. If your list of pessimists was easier to write and is the longer list, this workbook will help you to develop and maintain a positive attitude. A positive attitude will allow you to take charge of your life and live up to your full potential.

Research shows that the average human being speaks at a rate of 150 words per minute and thinks at a rate of 800 words per minute. Further research suggests that the average human being is awake an average of 16 hours a day. This means that a maximum of 144,000 words can be spoken by an individual on a given day. This also means that a maximum of 768,000 words can be thought by an individual on a given day. In total, words spoken and thought by an individual can equal 912,000. That's a lot of words. To begin to better monitor our spoken words and thoughts, let us take the following action step:

List fifty *optimistic* (positive) statements you spoke or thought recently:

1. _____

_____

2. _____

_____

3. _____

_____

4. _____

_____

5. _____

_____

6. _____

_____

7. _____

_____

8. _____

_____

9. _____

_____

10. _____

_____

11. _____

_____

12. _____

_____

13. _____

_____

14. _____

_____

15. _____

_____

16. _____

_____

17. _____

_____

18. _____

_____

19. _____

_____

20. _____

_____

21. _____

_____

22. _____

_____

23. _____

_____

24. _____

_____

25. _____

_____

26. _____

_____

27. _____

_____

28. _____

_____

29. _____

_____

30. _____

_____

31. _____

_____

32. _____

_____

33. _____

_____

34. _____

_____

35. _____

_____

36. _____

_____

37. _____

_____

38. _____

_____

39. _____

_____

40. _____

_____

41. _____

_____

42. _____

_____

43. _____

_____

44. _____

_____

45. _____

_____

46. _____

_____

47. _____

_____

48. _____

_____

49. _____

_____

50. _____

_____

List fifty *pessimistic* (negative) statements you spoke or thought recently:

1. _____

_____

2. _____

_____

3. _____

_____

4. _____

_____

5. _____

_____

6. _____

_____

7. _____

_____

8. _____

_____

9. _____

_____

10. _____

_____

11. _____

_____

12. _____

_____

13. _____

_____

14. _____

_____

15. _____

_____

16. _____

_____

17. _____

_____

18. _____

_____

19. _____

_____

20. _____

_____

21. _____

_____

22. _____

_____

23. _____

_____

24. _____

_____

25. _____

_____

26. _____

_____

27. _____

_____

28. _____

_____

29. _____

_____

30. _____

_____

31. _____

_____

32. _____

_____

33. _____

_____

34. _____

_____

35. _____

_____

36. _____

_____

37. _____

_____

38. _____

_____

39. _____

_____

40. _____

_____

41. _____

_____

42. _____

_____

43. _____

_____

44. _____

_____

45. _____

_____

46. _____

_____

47. _____

_____

48. _____

_____

49. _____

_____

50. _____

_____

When you listed the fifty optimistic (positive) statements and fifty pessimistic (negative) statements, which of the two lists was easier to write?

Optimistic _____   Pessimistic _____

Of the fifty optimistic (positive) statements and fifty pessimistic (negative) statements you listed, which of the two lists is longer?

Optimistic _____   Pessimistic _____

Whichever list was easier to write and/or the longer, serves as a representation of your attitude. If your list of optimistic statements was the easier to write and/or the longer list, you probably have a positive attitude that simply needs to be tuned up. If your list of pessimistic statements was the easier to write and/or the longer list, you probably have a less than positive attitude. You need to develop a positive attitude and learn the tune-up tools required to maintain it.

To reframe your mental process, review the pessimistic (negative) statements you listed. Restate each pessimistic (negative) statement as an optimistic (positive) statement. Practice translating the negative words you speak and think daily into positive words.

1. _____

_____

2. _____

_____

3. _____

_____

4. _____

_____

5. _____

_____

6. _____

_____

7. _____

_____

8. _____

_____

9. _____

_____

10. _____

_____

11. _____

_____

12. _____

_____

13. _____

_____

14. _____

_____

15. _____

_____

16. _____

_____

17. _____

_____

18. _____

_____

19. _____

_____

20. _____

_____

21. _____

_____

22. _____

_____

23. _____

_____

24. _____

_____

25. _____

_____

26. _____

_____

27. _____

_____

28. _____

_____

29. _____

_____

30. _____

_____

31. _____

_____

32. _____

_____

33. _____

_____

34. _____

_____

35. _____

_____

36. _____

_____

37. _____

_____

38. _____

_____

39. _____

_____

40. _____

_____

41. _____

_____

42. _____

_____

43. _____

_____

44. _____

_____

45. _____

_____

46. _____

_____

47. _____

_____

48. _____

_____

49. _____

_____

50. _____

_____

We have a choice wherein we can choose to respond to our challenges rather than react to them. The definition of reaction is a reverse action or countermeasure taken against some influence or event. Why is the definition of reaction *a reverse action*? When we react to a challenge we are at the mercy of our external challenge. Challenges have the tendency to "set us back." In reaction to our challenges we then "bounce back." Our society deems this as appropriate behavior. It is not! The formula of *(a)* challenges appear and set us back, *(b)* we react to the challenges and hopefully bounce back is an incorrect formula. This is not having control over your life. This is not having control over your circumstances. Your circumstances are in control of you.

The definition of response is to make a return by some action as if in answer to an influence or event. Why is the definition of response *a return*? When we respond to a challenge we take control over our lives. We zap the energy and power out of our challenges by responding to them. The key word *return* in the definition or response suggests that the person faced with the challenge must go somewhere. As you will learn later in this workbook, we teach that all meaningful change comes from within. What people who respond to a challenge must do is go within. They would use all the tools and techniques that are in this workbook that are applicable to their challenge. After having done their inner work, they would *return* to the challenge and overcome it. This is having control over your life. This is having control over your circumstances. This is the formula that works!

I want to give you several opportunities to have your attitude assessed.

Peer assessments: On pages 30–32 you will find a peer-assessment sheet. Make four to six copies of this sheet. Prepare four to six self-addressed, stamped envelopes. With copies and envelopes in hand, ask four to six co-workers, friends, and/or family members to participate in this exercise by providing you with anonymous feedback. Emphasize that you are requiring your peers to mail their responses to you anonymously in an attempt to increase the probability of receiving honest and accurate feedback. Request that your peers complete and mail their assessments no later than twenty-four hours after they receive it. Repeat this process periodically to measure your growth. Assessments are critical to the attitude-building process.

Self-assessment: Following the peer assessment you will find an attitude self-assessment (pages 33–35). Make four copies of this sheet. I encourage you to take the attitude self-assessment periodically to measure your growth. Please follow the instructions and answer each question honestly and to the best of your ability.

Score your assessments: Following the attitude self-assessment you will find an attitude-assessment score sheet (pages 35–37). Use this sheet to score both your peer assessments and your attitude self-assessment. List each score below. Compare your peer-assessment scores to your attitude self-assessment score. Repeat this process periodically to measure your growth.

Peer-Assessment Scores: (1)___67___ (2)___69___ (3)___72___
(4)___68___ (5)___66___ (6)___72___
Self-Assessment Score: ___72___

If you would like, total all your peer-assessment scores and your self-assessment score to create a cumulative score. Divide the cumulative score by the total number of assessments to identify your average attitude-assessment score. Periodically repeat this process to measure your overall growth.

Cumulative Score: 67 + 69 + 72 + 68 + 66 + 72 + 72 = 486
Average Attitude-Assessment Score: 486 / 7 = 69.42
Peer-Assessment Scores: (1) _____ (2) _____ (3) _____ (4) _____
(5) _____ (6) _____
Self-Assessment Score: _____
Cumulative Score: _____   Average Attitude-Assessment Score: _____

ATTITUDE PEER ASSESSMENT

Please check the column that best describes your assessment of your peer.

	ALMOST ALWAYS	SOMETIMES	ALMOST NEVER
1. He/She can identify opportunities in new situations	_____	_____	_____

	ALMOST ALWAYS	SOMETIMES	ALMOST NEVER
2. He/She is doubtful of new situations until they've been proven	_____	_____	_____
3. He/She fears there's nothing better than his/her current situation	_____	_____	_____
4. He/She won't be able to handle change	_____	_____	_____
5. He/She will do well when a new situation is clear	_____	_____	_____
6. He/She is trusting of those responsible for implementing change	_____	_____	_____
7. He/She can't wait to see what's in store for each new day	_____	_____	_____
8. He/She feels like things are too good to be true, and will certainly change today	_____	_____	_____
9. He/She is never certain he/she will get done what needs to get done today	_____	_____	_____
10. He/She is confident the things he/she needs to get done today will get done— and done well	_____	_____	_____

	ALMOST ALWAYS	SOMETIMES	ALMOST NEVER
11. He/She is just going through the motions and in need of something to happen to change things	_____	_____	_____
12. He/She is secure in his/her job and appears to be doing OK	_____	_____	_____
13. He/She looks forward to finding new opportunities each new day	_____	_____	_____
14. He/She has a good attitude	_____	_____	_____
15. He/She doesn't allow the little things to bother him/her	_____	_____	_____
16. His/Her enthusiasm toward his/her life and job has been high the last few weeks	_____	_____	_____
17. He/She has a positive attitude	_____	_____	_____
18. His/Her attitude would be rated as positive by others	_____	_____	_____
19. He/She has had no problem treating others with patience and sensitivity lately	_____	_____	_____
20. His/Her creativity level has been high in the last few weeks	_____	_____	_____

ATTITUDE SELF-ASSESSMENT

Please check the column that most closely describes your recent experiences, feelings, and attitudes involving each of the following statements:

	ALMOST ALWAYS	SOMETIMES	ALMOST NEVER
1. I can identify opportunities in new situations	_____	_____	_____
2. I am doubtful of new situations until they've been proven	_____	_____	_____
3. I fear there's nothing better than my current situation	_____	_____	_____
4. I am concerned that others won't be able to handle change	_____	_____	_____
5. I know I'll do well once a new situation is clear	_____	_____	_____
6. I trust those responsible for implementing change	_____	_____	_____
7. I can't wait to see what's in store for each new day	_____	_____	_____

	ALMOST ALWAYS	SOMETIMES	ALMOST NEVER
8. I feel like things are too good to be true, and will certainly change today	_____	_____	_____
9. I am not certain I'll get done what needs to get done today	_____	_____	_____
10. I am confident the things I need to get done today will get done—and done well	_____	_____	_____
11. I feel like I'm going through the motions and wish something would happen to change things	_____	_____	_____
12. I hope that my job is secure and my superiors think I'm doing OK	_____	_____	_____
13. I look forward to finding new opportunities each new day	_____	_____	_____
14. I feel my boss would say I have a good attitude	_____	_____	_____
15. I don't allow the little things to bother me	_____	_____	_____
16. I have had high enthusiasm toward my life and job in the last few weeks	_____	_____	_____

	ALMOST ALWAYS	SOMETIMES	ALMOST NEVER
17. I believe my co-workers and my family would say I have a positive attitue	_____	_____	_____
18. I would rate my attitude as positive	_____	_____	_____
19. I've had no problem treating others with patience and sensitivity lately	_____	_____	_____
20. I have had a high creativity level in the last few weeks	_____	_____	_____

SCORE YOUR ATTITUDE ASSESSMENT(S)

Circle the score that corresponds with the check mark on each column of each assessment. Add each column. Add the column totals. This is your score.

	ALMOST ALWAYS	SOMETIMES	ALMOST NEVER
1. I can identify opportunities in new situations	5	3	1
2. I am doubtful of new situations until they've been proven	1	3	5
3. I fear there's nothing better than my current situation	1	3	5

	ALMOST ALWAYS	SOMETIMES	ALMOST NEVER
4. I am concerned that others won't be able to handle change	1	3	5
5. I know I'll do well once a new situation is clear	5	3	1
6. I trust those responsible for implementing change	5	3	1
7. I can't wait to see what's in store for each new day	5	3	1
8. I feel like things are too good to be true, and will certainly change today	1	3	5
9. I am not certain I'll get done what needs to get done today	1	3	5
10. I am confident the things I need to get done today will get done—and done well	5	3	1
11. I feel like I'm going through the motions and wish something would happen to change things	1	3	5
12. I hope that my job is secure and my superiors think I'm doing OK	1	3	5
13. I look forward to finding new opportunities each new day	5	3	1

	ALMOST ALWAYS	SOMETIMES	ALMOST NEVER
14. I feel my boss would say I have a good attitude	5	3	1
15. I don't allow the little things to bother me	5	3	1
16. I have had high enthusiasm toward my life and job in the last few weeks	5	3	1
17. I believe my co-workers and my family would say I have a positive attitude	5	3	1
18. I would rate my attitude as positive	5	3	1
19. I've had no problem treating others with patience and sensitivity lately	5	3	1
20. I have had a high creativity level in the last few weeks	5	3	1

COLUMN TOTALS: _____ + _____ + _____

GRAND TOTAL: _____

RATE YOUR ATTITUDE

90–100 = A positive, proactive approach to most everything in your life! You have developed a positive mental attitude and only need to develop a process/system by which you can maintain your positive attitude. This workbook will help you achieve this objective.

70–89 = Generally have "good days and bad days." You will need to develop a mental perspective that will allow you to become positive and proactive more consistently. This workbook will help you tune up your attitude and it will teach you to develop a process/system wherein you can maintain the positive, proactive attitude you have worked to develop.

50–69 = Tendency to focus on the negative. Tuning up your attitude is a necessity! By investing your time tuning up your attitude, you too will develop a mental perspective that will allow you to become positive and proactive more consistently. By following the instructions in this workbook you will begin to develop a positive mental attitude. In time you will begin to observe the rewards of your newly developed perspective.

0–49 = The negative aspects of life pervade your thoughts and feelings. The tune-up exercises in this workbook will help you break through the pervasive negative thoughts and feelings that are currently holding you back. The instruction in this workbook will allow you to begin to realize the positive future ahead of you.

Take this time to set a practical goal for the attitude you desire to achieve in the near future. If your current score is 50–69, a practical goal would be to achieve a score of 70–89 first and then pursue the next highest score. Be sure to list a specific score and a specific date to achieve that score. Remember: *be practical!* You didn't develop your current attitude overnight and you won't develop your future attitude overnight either.

WRITE YOUR GOAL HERE!

I _____ on this _____ day of _____ set a goal of
(Your name)

achieving an average attitude-assessment score of _____ by
(Score range)

_____ .
(Date)

Signature: _____

Improving your attitude doesn't necessarily require making a 180-degree turn. Most of us are not 100 percent positive or negative all the time. Developing and maintaining a positive attitude is by no means black and white. There are a few shades of gray here and there. Optimists have bad days and pessimists have good days. Often we allow our attitudes to be affected by the events we experience day-to-day. "Life inflicts the same [difficulties] and tragedies on the optimist as on the pessimist, but the optimist weathers them better," writes psychologist Martin Seligman. If I had to summarize the complete, overall lesson of this workbook that would be it: teaching you to master the process of taking control of your responses to the events you experience day-to-day, and teaching you to maintain a positive attitude even when the events surrounding your life are not so positive. Showing you the power you have to take charge of your life.

What happens to you does not have to happen within you. Every one of us endures hardships that we allow to bring out the worst in us or inspire the best in us. It all comes down to which attitude you choose. When faced with a difficult challenge, you must focus on staying positive. You must recognize hardships and other challenges as opportunities to learn and to grow. When you commit yourself to focus on the possibilities of tomorrow, rather than allowing yourself to be bogged down by the realities of today, you will begin to experience the unlimited rewards associated with your positive mental attitude. It is a challenging process to unlearn your old thought processes and behaviors and learn new ones. We recognize this challenge and are doing everything we can to make this process as convenient, yet value added, for you as possible.

One of the first things we need to do to turn your attitude into action is to tap into the power of your attitude. This key step is the foundation on which the other nine steps are built. It is imperative that you understand the power of your attitude. Attitude is everything; it impacts everything you do! Attitude is the foundation and support of everything you do, a key element in the process of taking responsibility for and achieving mastery in your personal and professional life. Learning to develop and maintain a positive attitude is key to any self-help process; however, it isn't how much you know about developing and maintaining a positive attitude that's important—it's how well and how consistently you put that knowledge to use. I do not want you to simply make the content of this workbook a part of your common knowledge. I desire that you take the knowledge contained in this workbook, internalize it, and make it common practice every day and in everything you say and do. I've attended numerous seminars and have witnessed countless individuals who take the knowledge and run with it and become the better as a result of it; however, I have also witnessed others who take the knowledge and sit on it, and it in no way improves their life. It is a sad scenario that such a minor distinction in how individuals manage their knowledge can make such a massive difference in the end results.

Take the following action step: List twenty-five decisions you can make that will allow you to tap into the power of your positive attitude over the next seven days (week one). They do not have to be major decisions. Each decision should benefit yourself and at least one other person.

Examples:

1. Spending quality time with your children, helping with their homework, playing ball in the yard, etc.
2. Spending quality time with your mate, helping to prepare dinner or clean up after dinner, watching a favorite movie, taking a walk through the neighborhood, etc.
3. Deciding to call or write a friend or relative you have, by choice, not communicated with due to an unreconciled difference.
4. Deciding to volunteer for a day at a local community organization—school, church, charitable group, etc.

1. _____
2. _____
3. _____
4. _____
5. _____
6. _____
7. _____
8. _____
9. _____
10. _____
11. _____
12. _____
13. _____

14. _____

15. _____

16. _____

17. _____

18. _____

19. _____

20. _____

21. _____

22. _____

23. _____

24. _____

25. _____

Now that you've made your decisions, exercise the power of your attitude by enforcing each of your decisions with positive actions. What things must you do now, and in what attitude must they be done, in order to allow you to experience the power of your attitude? An example is: calling long-distance to speak with my brother John, whom I have not spoken to in several months because of a disagreement, and telling him I love him in an attitude of compassion and sincerity.

Positive action(s) for:

Decision 1. _____

_____

_____

Decision 2. _____

_____

_____

Decision 3. _____

_____

_____

Decision 4. _____

_____

_____

Decision 5. _____

_____

_____

Decision 6. _____

_____

_____

Decision 7. _____

_____

_____

Decision 8. _____

_____

_____

Decision 9. _____

_____

_____

Decision 10. _____

_____

_____

Decision 11. _____

_____

_____

Decision 12. _____

_____

_____

Decision 13. _____

_____

_____

Decision 14. _____

_____

_____

Decision 15. _____

_____

_____

Decision 16. _____

_____

_____

Decision 17. _____

_____

_____

Decision 18. _____

_____

_____

Decision 19. _____

_____

_____

Decision 20. _____

_____

_____

Decision 21. _____

_____

_____

Decision 22. _____

_____

_____

Decision 23. _____

_____

_____

Decision 24. _____

_____

_____

Decision 25. _____

_____

_____

By identifying twenty-five decisions, and taking the steps required to rein-force those decisions with positive actions, you have begun to understand the power of attitude. With this new understanding you can begin to develop the momentum necessary to activate the real driving force within you. This is essential to your success in the attitude-building process.

Now take the next step in the attitude-building process. Repeat the process over the next seven days (week two). Create a new list. Your new list may be a repeat of your old list, a completely new list, or a combination of the two. Repeat this process a third and a fourth time until you have completed four full weeks. At the end of the four weeks write how this process has made you and the others around you feel.

(Week 2)

1. _____

2. _____

3. _____

4. _____

5. _____

6. _____

7. _____

8. _____

9. _____

10. _____

11. _____

12. _____

13. _____

14. _____

15. _____

16. _____

17. _____

18. _____

19. _____

20. _____

21. _____

22. _____

23. _____

24. _____

25. _____

Positive action(s) for:

Decision 1. _____

_____

_____

Decision 2. _____

_____

_____

Decision 3. _____

_____

_____

Decision 4. _____

_____

_____

Decision 5. _____

_____

_____

Decision 6. _____

_____

_____

Decision 7. _____

_____

_____

Decision 8. _____

_____

_____

Decision 9. _____

_____

_____

Decision 10. _____

_____

_____

Decision 11. _____

_____

_____

Decision 12. _____

_____

_____

Decision 13. _____

_____

_____

Decision 14. _____

_____

_____

Decision 15. _____

_____

_____

Decision 16. _____

_____

_____

Decision 17. _____

_____

_____

Decision 18. _____

_____

_____

Decision 19. _____

_____

_____

Decision 20. _____

_____

_____

Decision 21. _____

_____

_____

Decision 22. _____

_____

_____

Decision 23. _____

_____

_____

Decision 24. _____

_____

_____

Decision 25. _____

_____

_____

(Week 3)

1. _____
2. _____
3. _____
4. _____

5. _____

6. _____

7. _____

8. _____

9. _____

10. _____

11. _____

12. _____

13. _____

14. _____

15. _____

16. _____

17. _____

18. _____

19. _____

20. _____

21. _____

22. _____

23. _____

24. _____

25. _____

Positive action(s) for:

Decision 1. _____

_____

_____

Decision 2. _____

_____

_____

Decision 3. _____

_____

_____

Decision 4. _____

_____

_____

Decision 5. _____

_____

_____

Decision 6. _____

_____

_____

Decision 7. _____

_____

_____

Decision 8. _____

_____

_____

Decision 9. _____

_____

_____

Decision 10. _____

_____

_____

Decision 11. _____

_____

_____

Decision 12. _____

_____

_____

Decision 13. _____

_____

_____

Decision 14. _____

_____

_____

Decision 15. _____

_____

_____

Decision 16. _____

_____

_____

Decision 17. _____

_____

_____

Decision 18. _____

_____

_____

Decision 19. _____

_____

_____

Decision 20. _____

_____

_____

Decision 21. _____

_____

_____

Decision 22. _____

_____

_____

Decision 23. _____

_____

_____

Decision 24. _____

_____

_____

Decision 25. _____

_____

_____

(Week 4)

1. _____
2. _____
3. _____
4. _____

5. _____

6. _____

7. _____

8. _____

9. _____

10. _____

11. _____

12. _____

13. _____

14. _____

15. _____

16. _____

17. _____

18. _____

19. _____

20. _____

21. _____

22. _____

23. _____

24. _____

25. _____

Positive action(s) for:

Decision 1. _____

_____

_____

Decision 2. _____

_____

_____

Decision 3. _____

_____

_____

Decision 4. _____

_____

_____

Decision 5. _____

_____

_____

Decision 6. _____

_____

_____

Decision 7. _____

_____

_____

Decision 8. _____

_____

_____

Decision 9. _____

_____

_____

Decision 10. _____

_____

_____

Decision 11. _____

_____

_____

Decision 12. _____

_____

_____

Decision 13. _____

_____

_____

Decision 14. _____

_____

_____

Decision 15. _____

_____

_____

Decision 16. _____

_____

_____

Decision 17. _____

_____

_____

Decision 18. _____

_____

_____

Decision 19. _____

_____

_____

Decision 20. _____

_____

_____

Decision 21. _____

_____

_____

Decision 22. _____

_____

_____

Decision 23. _____

_____

_____

Decision 24. _____

_____

_____

Decision 25. _____

_____

_____

How did the past four weeks make you and the others around you feel?

_____

_____

_____

_____

_____

_____

_____

_____

_____

_____

_____

_____

_____

_____

_____

_____

_____

_____

In life you do not get what you want, you get what you are. If you desire love, be loving. If you desire friendship, be a friend. If you desire a closer relationship with your mate, your children, or members of your extended family, do the things that will make it happen! Become that which you desire by making what you have accomplished in the previous exercise a part of your daily practice.

THE
ATTITUDE
IS
EVERYTHING
WORKBOOK

STEP II

"CHOOSE TO TAKE CHARGE OF YOUR LIFE"

You don't get to choose how you're going to die, or when. You can only choose how you're going to live.

—*Joan Baez*

HE LEGENDARY HARVARD psychologist and philosopher William James said that one of the most important discoveries made by his generation was that by changing our attitudes, we can change our lives. It's a choice we all have. The choices are sometimes basic. Something as simple as how you wake up in the morning is an example of the attitude you choose. Those with a positive attitude throw off their bedcovers each morning, climb out of bed enthusiastically, smile, and approach the day with positive expectation. Those with negative attitudes drag themselves out of bed, frown, grumble, and face the day with negative expectations. Sometimes the choices are far more complex. Something as complicated as the decision to live or die is an example of your attitude. As we will learn from the following stories, your attitude is your choice.

Melissa was in the retail clothing business. She was always in a good mood. She always had something positive to say. She was a unique manager because she inspired her employees and everyone who came into her store. She never had a bad day or a down moment. Melissa would always tell her employees to look on the positive side of every situation.

Every time I went into the store I noticed Melissa's upbeat, enthusiastic attitude. Irate customers didn't seem to affect her. She had smiles and kind words for everyone. So one day I went up to Melissa and said, "I don't get it. You can't be a positive person all the time. How do you do it?"

"Each morning I wake up and say to myself, 'Melissa, you have two choices. You can choose to be in a good mood, or you can choose to be in a bad mood.' I choose to be in a good mood. Each time something happens, I can choose to be a victim or I can choose to learn from it. I choose to learn from it. Every time someone comes in complaining, I can choose to accept their complaining or I can point out the positive side of life. I point out the positive side of life."

"It can't be that easy," I protested.

"Yes, it is," Melissa said. "Life is all about choices. When you cut away all the junk, every situation is a choice. You choose how you react to situations. You choose how people will affect your mood. You choose to be in a good mood or a bad mood. The bottom line: It's your choice how you live."

Several months after that conversation, I was in the mall and stopped by the store just to say hello to Melissa. She wasn't there. One of the employees informed me that she had been in a near fatal automobile accident. She had suffered internal bleeding, a punctured lung, a broken collarbone, and a broken leg.

After hours of surgery, weeks of intensive care, and months of physical therapy, Melissa was back at work. I saw her shortly after she returned and asked her how she was doing after such a challenging time. "I feel super fantastic," she replied.

When I asked her what she remembered about the accident, Melissa replied, "I remembered that I had two choices: I could choose to live or I could choose to die. I chose to live." Melissa's attitude demonstrates for us that every day we have a choice about how we're going to live our lives.

Studies have been conducted to determine how optimistic attitudes can affect cancer patients, HIV patients, and stroke victims treated by physicians. The conclusions show that patients with a positive outlook experienced overall better health, less stress, and longer lives.

Researchers from the M.D. Anderson Center in Houston, Texas, conducted studies to determine how optimistic attitudes can affect depression and stress levels in cancer patients. Results from the study proved patients with a positive outlook experienced lower levels of stress and depression during their treatment process.

Similar studies on HIV patients and stroke victims provide almost identical outcomes. Optimism has been linked to slower progression of symptoms and longer life among men with HIV. Research shows that stroke victims with pessimistic attitudes are 58 percent more likely to die compared to optimistic victims. The power of attitude is phenomenal!

As the winner of the world and U.S. pro cycling championships, Lance Armstrong was a twenty-five-year-old rising star on the international circuit. Then, in 1996, he discovered that a particularly deadly form of cancer had spread from his testicles to his stomach, lungs, and brain. Doctors said he had only a 50 percent chance of surviving. His racing career was put on hold for more than a year while he underwent intensive chemotherapy.

Someone who felt helpless about controlling his attitude probably would have plunged into depression or despair and given up. But Lance Armstrong amazed his doctors and much of the world by not letting his extreme circumstances defeat him. Instead, he got back on his bicycle and continued to train during his treatments, sometimes riding as much as fifty miles a day.

Although others might have chosen an attitude of helplessness, despair, or defeat, Lance Armstrong chose a combative attitude toward the disease that threatened his life. It's true that many people have fought cancer bravely and still lost out in spite of courageous efforts. But for reasons that even his doctors have not yet determined, Armstrong won his battle against cancer. His cancer disappeared entirely. Lance Armstrong's story is but a single example of one of the greatest gifts God has given us—the freedom to choose!

Think of your mind as a computer that can be programmed. You can choose whether the software that is installed is productive or unproductive to your quality of life. Your inner dialogue is the software that programs your attitude, which determines how you present yourself to the world around you. You have control over what that programming is. Whatever you put into it is reflected in what comes out.

Most people allow their brains to be programmed indiscriminately. The computer adage "Garbage in, garbage out," as it applies to our own very personal computer—the brain—should be stated as "Garbage in, garbage stays and attracts more garbage." The same is true of people who program their brains discriminately, filling their very personal computers—their brains—with positive, valuable content. For them it can be stated as "Nourishing thoughts in, nourishing thoughts stay and attract more nourishing thoughts."

My friend Scott and his mother, Lela, lived in Miami, Florida, when Hurricane Andrew devastated the area in August of 1992. Lela prayed the night prior to the hurricane as she did every night before going to bed. It was her belief that if she planted the seeds of a positive attitude in her mind every night prior to going to bed, she would reap the harvest of her positive attitude in the form of an improved quality of life each day. Very much aware of the news reports of the impending danger of Hurricane Andrew, Lela prayed and she went to sleep. Scott remained awake, vigilant, and prepared to respond to the approaching hurricane in any way that would ensure his and his mother's safety.

At 4:05 A.M. Scott woke his mother, removed her from her room, and positioned both his mother and himself in a small closet. After hours of waiting in nearly two inches of water, they heard windows explode due to an increase in air pressure, heard furniture hit the walls as hurricane winds blew fiercely through their home, heard the interior roof cave in due to water retention in the attic, heard everything, yet were unable to see anything. When they surfaced from what proved to be a truly secure place in their home, Scott and Lela discovered that Hurricane Andrew had destroyed their home and all its contents.

Scott climbed over the debris to check on neighbors. When he returned to his devastated home he found his mother, Lela, standing in what remained of the kitchen, cooking breakfast. Though the hurricane had destroyed the cabinets, windows, and the door of the kitchen, the gas range was still securely connected to the gas line. And although the refrigerator was virtually lying on its side, much of the food in the refrigerator had not spilled or spoiled. In the midst of this horrendous tragedy Lela cooked breakfast for her elderly neighbors and neighborhood children. Scott searched through the debris in the vicinity of the kitchen and found clean disposable plates and plastic eating utensils wrapped in plastic storage bags.

Lela is proof that it's not what happens to us that matters, it's how we choose to respond. Lela discriminately planted the seeds of a positive mental attitude in her mind and resolved that no matter what happened around her, she was going to experience an improved quality of life. She did just that in spite of losing her home of nearly forty years and the contents of her home she had sacrificed for years to acquire. Her positive attitude was so powerful that it positively influenced Scott's attitude and enabled him to cope through this challenging and difficult time as well.

Like Lela you have the power to choose the attitude you will have every morning you wake up. That predetermined attitude will influence your behavior for the entire day, maybe your entire life. One of the keys to improving the quality of your life is your willingness to exercise your power to choose your attitude and your approach to life's challenges. Taking charge and staying in control is an attitude of choice. If Lela could overcome Hurricane Andrew with a positive attitude, after having lost every material possession she owned, surely you can overcome divorce, being downsized from a job, the loss of a loved one, an unhealthy relationship, failing at a business venture, etc. Whatever your current challenge is, you can overcome it with the "right" attitude!

List ten challenges you currently face:*

1. _____

2. _____

3. _____

4. _____

5. _____

6. _____

7. _____

8. _____

9. _____

10. _____

*Note: Keep these ten challenges foremost in your mind as you complete this workbook.

The following activities are designed to help you begin to recognize how the attitude you choose *today* impacts the challenges you face *today* and the quality of your life *forevermore!*

Below you will find a thirty-one-day journal. For thirty-one consecutive days select three individual words that describe your attitude (your frame of mind or your disposition) each morning when you awake. Write how you actually feel. An individual word description of how you feel on a particular morning can be: great, energetic, tired, frustrated, depressed, angry, happy, excited, motivated, ill, discouraged, inspired, anxious, helpless, free, beautiful, ugly, good, caring, loving, hateful, guilty, giving, rich, poor, powerful, weak, vulnerable, etc. Once you select your daily descriptions, identify the event(s) you believe contribute to the attitude you describe. Last, write a description of how you choose to feel. At the end of each description write these words: "My life is not over. I have the power to make of my life what I choose."

Example:

Day 1:

Description 1. Tired _____

Event(s) I am tired because I worked a double last night and did not

get enough sleep. _____

Description 2. Frustrated

Event(s) I am frustrated because I am tired of working so hard just

to survive.

Description 3. Angry

Event(s) I am angry at myself for not doing more with my life.

I choose to feel refreshed, fulfilled, and at peace. My life is not over.

I have the power to make of my life what I choose.

Day 1:

Description 1.

Event(s)

Description 2.

Event(s)

Description 3.

Event(s)

I choose to feel

Day 2:

Description 1. _____

Event(s) _____

Description 2. _____

Event(s) _____

Description 3. _____

Event(s) _____

I choose to feel _____

_____

Day 3:

Description 1. _____

Event(s) _____

Description 2. _____

Event(s) _____

Description 3. _____

Event(s) _____

I choose to feel _____

_____

Day 4:

Description 1. _____

Event(s) _____

Description 2. _____

Event(s) _____

Description 3. _____

Event(s) _____

I choose to feel _____

_____

Day 5:

Description 1. _____

Event(s) _____

Description 2. _____

Event(s) _____

Description 3. _____

Event(s) _____

I choose to feel _____

_____

Day 6:

Description 1. _____

Event(s) _____

Description 2. _____

Event(s) _____

Description 3. _____

Event(s) _____

I choose to feel _____

_____

Day 7:

Description 1. _____

Event(s) _____

Description 2. _____

Event(s) _____

Description 3. _____

Event(s) _____

I choose to feel _____

_____

Day 8:

Description 1. _____

Event(s) _____

Description 2. _____

Event(s) _____

Description 3. _____

Event(s) _____

I choose to feel _____

_____

Day 9:

Description 1. _____

Event(s) _____

Description 2. _____

Event(s) _____

Description 3. _____

Event(s) _____

I choose to feel _____

_____

Day 10:

Description 1. _____

Event(s) _____

Description 2. _____

Event(s) _____

Description 3. _____

Event(s) _____

I choose to feel _____

_____

Day 11:

Description 1. _____

Event(s) _____

Description 2. _____

Event(s) _____

Description 3. _____

Event(s) _____

I choose to feel _____

_____

Day 12:

Description 1. _____

Event(s) _____

Description 2. _____

Event(s) _____

Description 3. _____

Event(s) _____

I choose to feel _____

_____

Day 13:

Description 1. _____

Event(s) _____

Description 2. _____

Event(s) _____

Description 3. _____

Event(s) _____

I choose to feel _____

_____

Day 14:

Description 1. _____

Event(s) _____

Description 2. _____

Event(s) _____

Description 3. _____

Event(s) _____

I choose to feel _____

_____

Day 15:

Description 1. _____

Event(s) _____

Description 2. _____

Event(s) _____

Description 3. _____

Event(s) _____

I choose to feel _____

_____

Day 16:

Description 1. _____

Event(s) _____

Description 2. _____

Event(s) _____

Description 3. _____

Event(s) _____

I choose to feel _____

_____

Day 17:

Description 1. _____

Event(s) _____

Description 2. _____

Event(s) _____

Description 3. _____

Event(s) _____

I choose to feel _____

_____

Day 18:

Description 1. _____

Event(s) _____

Description 2. _____

Event(s) _____

Description 3. _____

Event(s) _____

I choose to feel _____

_____

Day 19:

Description 1. _____

Event(s) _____

Description 2. _____

Event(s) _____

Description 3. _____

Event(s) _____

I choose to feel _____

_____

Day 20:

Description 1. _____

Event(s) _____

Description 2. _____

Event(s) _____

Description 3. _____

Event(s) _____

I choose to feel _____

_____

Day 21:

Description 1. _____

Event(s) _____

Description 2. _____

Event(s) _____

Description 3. _____

Event(s) _____

I choose to feel _____

_____

Day 22:

Description 1. _____

Event(s) _____

Description 2. _____

Event(s) _____

Description 3. _____

Event(s) _____

I choose to feel _____

_____

Day 23:

Description 1. _____

Event(s) _____

Description 2. _____

Event(s) _____

Description 3. _____

Event(s) _____

I choose to feel _____

_____

Day 24:

Description 1. _____

Event(s) _____

Description 2. _____

Event(s) _____

Description 3. _____

Event(s) _____

I choose to feel _____

_____

Day 25:

Description 1. _____

Event(s) _____

Description 2. _____

Event(s) _____

Description 3. _____

Event(s) _____

I choose to feel _____

_____

Day 26:

Description 1. _____

Event(s) _____

Description 2. _____

Event(s) _____

Description 3. _____

Event(s) _____

I choose to feel _____

_____

Day 27:

Description 1. _____

Event(s) _____

Description 2. _____

Event(s) _____

Description 3. _____

Event(s) _____

I choose to feel _____

_____

Day 28:

Description 1. _____

Event(s) _____

Description 2. _____

Event(s) _____

Description 3. _____

Event(s) _____

I choose to feel _____

_____

Day 29:

Description 1. _____

Event(s) _____

Description 2. _____

Event(s) _____

Description 3. _____

Event(s) _____

I choose to feel _____

_____

Day 30:

Description 1. _____

Event(s) _____

Description 2. _____

Event(s) _____

Description 3. _____

Event(s) _____

I choose to feel _____

_____

Day 31:

Description 1. _____

Event(s) _____

Description 2. _____

Event(s) _____

Description 3. _____

Event(s) _____

I choose to feel _____

_____

By now you should be more aware and confident of the fact that your attitude is your choice and external events pale in comparison to your inner power to choose a positive attitude. By choosing to change your focus from external influences to nourishing and positive internal influences you take control of your attitude. You can choose to feel super fantastic every day—no matter what happens around you!

I woke up one morning and realized I was running late. I had to get to the airport to catch a flight. I drove seventy-five to eighty miles per hour to Hartsfield International. I ran up to the ticket counter and told the clerk I was late: *"Quick, I've got to catch the plane to San Francisco. Tell me the gate number."*

"You're going out of Concourse D. You've only got fifteen minutes," he said. "I don't think you're going to make it."

"I'm not going to make it talking to you, so would you please give me my ticket!"

I had a choice about how I would react to this situation. We all have a choice about how we react to each and every situation in our lives. Sometimes people tell you what you can't do because they don't see themselves achieving it. But the magic of the word *triumph* is in the first syllable. You've got to try.

I snatched that ticket and started running. I made it through security relatively fast. In the Atlanta airport, there's a train you have to catch to get to the concourse. I was running so fast I didn't have to catch the train. I wasn't just running. I was talking to myself too. *"Come on, you've got to go. You can't miss this flight. You've got to get there."* I was moving. I hit the escalator and never stopped running. My inner voice said, *"Boy you're out of shape. You'd better start working out."*

When I finally approached the gate, I noticed that the plane was still there. An airline agent was at the gate. *"Excuse me, ma'am,"* I said. *"I ran all the way from the ticket counter. Did I make it?"*

She responded, "We just got a phone call, the plane's going to be two hours delayed."

I looked at her and I said, *"That's OK. I'm positive and proactive."*

She said, "I don't care what you call yourself. We're not leaving for two hours."

As I started to walk away, I saw another gentleman come up behind me and approach the counter. He appeared to be a top-level executive. He said, "Excuse me, ma'am, is the flight leaving on time?" She told him they were having mechanical difficulties and that the flight would be leaving in two hours. He became angry. "Mechanical difficulties! Do you know whom you're talking to? I'm a million-miler-flying colonel. I know the CEO personally. I want to speak to your supervisor right now."

A supervisor in a nice red jacket appeared. This guy argued with her for thirty-five minutes. Can you guess what time the plane left? Two hours later. I guarantee you, nobody wanted to sit next to him. This fellow had another choice. He could have accepted the delay and made constructive use of his time.

The difference in our attitudes that day made the difference in our behaviors. I don't know that the executive suffered any serious consequences as a result of his anger, but I do know that he didn't accomplish anything positive, because he let his circumstances control his attitude.

I thought about the positive things I could do. How could I reframe this situation? I went and got something to eat—a grilled chicken sandwich and a large orange juice. I went to the bookstore and bought a book, Norman Vincent Peale's *Enthusiasm Makes the Difference.* I read chapter one right in the airport. Then I did something special. I believe that any time you're going through something, you've always got to go inward to find out what little things you can do to bring joy to your life. I love popcorn. If you ever see me in an airport, you'll always find me looking for the popcorn. If you're ever in Atlanta, Concourse D, it's Gate 19, $1.58 a box. I went and bought a box of popcorn.

Then I did something extra special. I called my grandma. Any time I'm going through something and I need a pick-me-up, all I've got to do is call Grandma. She lives in Seattle. After a fifteen-minute conversation with my grandma, I forgot all about the flight being late. It didn't even matter.

If you can visualize me going back to the gate, I'm smiling and whistling.

I've had something to eat, read chapter one of a great book, had some popcorn, and talked to my grandma. When I returned to the gate, I looked at the passengers waiting for the flight, and some of them looked extremely toxic. I truly believe the toxic attitudes rub off, and exposure to them, over a period of time, might damage my attitude.

I scanned the area, chose a seat, and sat down next to a gentleman. I was just sitting there eating my popcorn, minding my own business. The man sitting next to me looked at me and asked, "Why are you so happy? Don't you know we've been here for an hour and a half? We've got another thirty minutes to go."

I responded, *"I have a choice and I'm choosing to be positive."*

He said, "Positive about what?"

I looked at him and stated, *"Let me give you three reasons. This flight is delayed either because there is something wrong with the plane, something wrong with the weather, or something wrong with the pilot. In case any of those three scenarios are true, I'm happy to be sitting here talking to you. I'd rather be here wishing I was up there than to be up there wishing I was down here."*

He looked at me, smiled, and said, "You've got a point. So how about sharing some of that popcorn?"

In the world of race car driving, when new drivers are learning how to race, they are taught what to do when they go into a spin while traveling at speeds that sometimes exceed 200 mph. The natural tendency is for drivers to focus on the wall they're trying to avoid hitting—and they usually end up hitting the wall. Instead they are taught not to focus on the wall, but to focus on where they want to go. By focusing on where they want to go they increase their chances of avoiding the wall and successfully getting out of the spin and finishing the race. The same is true for you. When life's challenges come your way and you feel yourself or the events around you spinning out of control, wherever you place your focus, positive or negative, that's the attitude that's going to produce the final result. I encourage you to maintain a positive focus. Search to find the good in everything.

Focus on where you want to go, what you want the outcome to be, in spite of the appearance of your current circumstances.

I asked you to keep the ten challenges you are currently facing foremost in your mind. Go back and review those current challenges. What do you desire the outcome of those challenges to be? What must you begin to focus on to make your desire a reality? What attitude must you begin to develop to achieve the end result you desire? What must you do to accomplish the outcome you desire?

There is a fictional story about a set of identical twins named Seymour and Fillmore that further demonstrates the effect of focus on one's attitude. Seymour was an unwavering optimist. Every night he went to bed with these words: "I can't wait until tomorrow!" Fillmore was sad by comparison. He always looked for the black cloud over the silver lining. He even considered his name to be an indication that he'd been born half empty.

Since the boys were supposed to be identical twins, their parents grew concerned at the disparity in their personalities and took them to a psychologist. He suggested that the parents work at balancing out the twins' divergent personalities at their next cobirthday party: "Buy Fillmore the best gift you can afford and give it to him in his room. Give Seymour a box of horse manure and give it to him in the backyard," advised the psychologist.

The parents followed the psychologist's instructions and carefully observed the results. When they took Fillmore to his room to see his gift, they heard his usual griping, even though they'd given him a state-of-the-art personal computer. "I wanted a laptop, not a PC," he complained.

Next they took Seymour outside to open his gift. Holding their noses at the stink of his gift, they were amazed as Seymour opened the gift and began merrily digging through the box of horse manure with his hands and crying out joyfully, "This is great! With all this manure there has to be a pony around here somewhere!"

That's the power of a positive attitude! While we have little control over the events in our lives, we do have control over our responses to those events. Simple awareness can break the pattern of allowing your unconscious to control your attitude. Make a conscious, deliberate decision daily to focus on the positive. No matter what challenges you experience, always find a minimum of two things positive about the situation.

This is how you transform your attitude into action—accept responsibility for what you choose to focus on when events happen in your life. Choose a nourishing, positive attitude by focusing on the positive. Commit yourself to the 5 percent and 95 percent rule. Direct no more than 5 percent of your focus on what you don't want and 95 percent on what you do want.

In this chapter we had you journalize your state of mind or how you actually felt for thirty-one days. We also had you journalize how you chose to feel. From this day forward, continue to acknowledge your state of mind or feelings; however, choose to focus on how you choose to feel. By focusing on how you choose to feel you alter your state of mind or feelings to match your focus.

When you feel stressed, don't speak it. When you feel tired, don't speak it. When you are experiencing any negative state of mind or feeling, do not speak it. It will keep you in that state of mind. Speak positive words and think positive thoughts. Your unconscious mind will begin to influence your conscious mind and your positive focus will begin to produce positive results.

For the next thirty-one mornings journalize how you choose to feel each day. Get in the habit of waking up, going to your workbook, and journalizing how you choose to feel each day.

Day 1:

I choose to feel _____

_____

Day 2:

I choose to feel _____

_____

Day 3:

I choose to feel _____

_____

Day 4:

I choose to feel _____

_____

Day 5:

I choose to feel _____

_____

Day 6:

I choose to feel _____

_____

Day 7:

I choose to feel _____

_____

Day 8:

I choose to feel _____

_____

Day 9:

I choose to feel _____

_____

Day 10:

I choose to feel _____

_____

Day 11:

I choose to feel _____

_____

Day 12:

I choose to feel _____

_____

Day 13:

I choose to feel _____

_____

Day 14:

I choose to feel _____

_____

Day 15:

I choose to feel _____

_____

Day 16:

I choose to feel _____

_____

Day 17:

I choose to feel _____

_____

Day 18:

I choose to feel _____

_____

Day 19:

I choose to feel _____

_____

Day 20:

I choose to feel _____

_____

Day 21:

I choose to feel _____

_____

Day 22:

I choose to feel _____

_____

Day 23:

I choose to feel _____

_____

Day 24:

I choose to feel _____

_____

Day 25:

I choose to feel _____

_____

Day 26:

I choose to feel _____

_____

Day 27:

I choose to feel _____

_____

Day 28:

I choose to feel _____

_____

Day 29:

I choose to feel _____

_____

Day 30:

I choose to feel _____

_____

Day 31:

I choose to feel _____

_____

Focus on how you choose to feel each morning. Choosing a positive mental attitude each morning will impact your entire day. Each positive day will result in a positive internal quality of life that supersedes any external challenges you may encounter. Who you are and what you believe on the inside impacts what you experience as reality on the outside.

STEP III

"A GOOD ATTITUDE BEGINS WITH SELF-AWARENESS"

First say to yourself what you would be;
and then do what you have to do.

—*Epictetus*

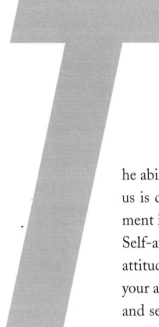

he ability to recognize our feelings as they quickly come over us is called self-awareness, and it is critical to our development in a highly mobile, fast changing, and complex society. Self-awareness allows you to be aware of your emotions and attitudes. Knowing yourself and understanding what drives your attitude and emotions is the first step to self-knowledge and self-control. If you remember the experiences that trigger a bad or self-destructive attitude, you can then work to disarm those triggers and even replace the bad emotions with more constructive and empowering emotions to create a better attitude.

Self-awareness is very important. When you tell yourself *I shouldn't be saying or doing this or thinking about that*, you are practicing self-awareness because you are monitoring your emotions and judging their potential impact.

When you practice self-awareness, you give yourself far greater control of your actions. This control gives you options. You can decide not to react to negative emotions. Instead you can develop a positive attitude that allows you to let go of the emotion. You can also channel the energy of the negative emotion into a positive action.

Do you become easily angered, impatient, insecure, or cynical for reasons you don't understand? Do other people tell you that you tend to overreact? Do you often find yourself wondering why you got so upset—so angry? So offended? It may be that you have an attitude that you need to examine and root out.

Attitude consists primarily of your disposition, frame of mind, perspective, and/or demeanor. Self-awareness allows us to take control of our attitudes by allowing us to uncover where those attitudes originate. To allow you to become self-aware of your current attitude complete the following fifty statements, beginning each statement with the words "I am . . ." List your thoughts, whether they are positive or negative.

Example: I am a happy person.

1. _____

2. _____

3. _____

4. _____

5. _____

6. _____

7. _____

8. _____

9. _____

10. _____

11. _____

12. _____

13. _____

14. _____

15. _____

16. _____

17. _____

18. _____

19. _____

20. _____

21. _____

22. _____

23. _____

24. _____

25. _____

26. _____

27. _____

28. _____

29. _____

30. _____

31. _____

32. _____

33. _____

34. _____

35. _____

36. _____

37. _____

38. _____

39. _____

40. _____

41. _____

42. _____

43. _____

44. _____

45. _____

46. _____

47. _____

48. _____

49. _____

50. _____

To understand how you developed your current attitude, review the fifty "I am . . ." statements. For each statement, identify the first time you remember someone describing you in that way. List the person's relationship to you.

1. _____

2. _____

3. _____

4. _____

5. _____

6. _____

7. _____

8. _____

9. _____

10. _____

11. _____

12. _____

13. _____

14. _____

15. _____

16. _____

17. _____

18. _____

19. _____

20. _____

21. _____

22. _____

23. _____

24. _____

25. _____

26. _____

27. _____

28. _____

29. _____

30. _____

31. _____

32. _____

33. _____

34. _____

35. _____

36. _____

37. _____

38. _____

39. _____

40. _____

41. _____

42. _____

43. _____

44. _____

45. _____

46. _____

47. _____

48. _____

49. _____

50. _____

Review the fifty "I am . . ." statements. For each statement, identify others you have heard use those words to describe you in the last month and their relationship to you.

1. _____

2. _____

3. _____

4. _____

5. _____

6. _____

7. _____

8. _____

9. _____

10. _____

11. _____

12. _____

13. _____

14. _____

15. _____

16. _____

17. _____

18. _____

19. _____

20. _____

21. _____

22. _____

23. _____

24. _____

25. _____

26. _____

27. _____

28. _____

29. _____

30. _____

31. _____

32. _____

33. _____

34. _____

35. _____

36. _____

37. _____

38. _____

39. _____

40. _____

41. _____

42. _____

43. _____

44. _____

45. _____

46. _____

47. _____

48. _____

49. _____

50. _____

Write about your earliest remembrance of each description. Write how the descriptions made you feel then and how they make you feel now. Write how those descriptions have impacted your current attitude toward yourself and others. Begin with your earliest remembrance. Proceed until you arrive at your most recent remembrance.

Example: At a very young age I recall being picked on and told I could not talk because I stuttered badly. I recall being insecure when asked to speak back then; however, years later and even now I feel empowered after overcoming that challenge. The feeling of insecurity has been replaced with a feeling of great confidence, so much so that professional speaking is my full-time job.

_____

_____

_____

_____

_____

_____

_____

_____

_____

_____

_____

_____

_____

_____

_____

_____

_____

_____

_____

_____

_____

_____

_____

_____

_____

_____

_____

_____

_____

_____

_____

_____

_____

_____

_____

_____

_____

_____

We are not permanently burdened with the baggage of our pasts. We can choose to leave that luggage behind. It's OK to clean out the suitcases and take the good stuff that fits us well—the happy memories, the lessons learned, the joy of a first love. But the rest of it—the sad times, the loneliness, the broken heart, rejection, fear—you no longer need that emotional baggage. It will only mess up your attitude and your life. Leave it and step into a brand-new future. History does not have to repeat itself, not if you adjust your attitude by turning away from the doors that are closed and walking through the doors that are opened to opportunity. There are three types of "attitude baggage" we must consider:

1. If-Only *Baggage (Past)*

The first piece of bad attitude baggage many people carry around is marked *If only.* This is baggage that has to do with the past. It is often full of unfinished business, plans that didn't turn out right, or hurt feelings that have not healed. It's heavy stuff. The following are some of the things typically found in the *If-only* baggage:

If only:

- *I'd thought before I said . . .*
- *I hadn't had that last drink.*
- *I'd stayed in school.*
- *I'd listened to . . .*
- *I'd been more careful.*
- *I'd spent more time with . . .*
- *I'd put more effort into the relationship.*
- *I'd managed my money better.*
- *I'd planned for my future sooner.*
- *I hadn't taken [a loved one] for granted.*

The *If-only* baggage gets heavier over time because it keeps growing and growing if you don't let it go. Unless you learn to release the past, you'll eventually become so bogged down by it that you'll never move ahead.

List your *If-only* baggage here:

_____

_____

_____

_____

_____

2. What-Now *Baggage (Present)*

This emotional baggage is packed under pressure of the present. It is heavy with stress and weighty expectations. It sometimes comes packed with good news as well as bad news, but the person carrying it chooses a negative response rather than a positive one. As a result, otherwise able-bodied men and women become paralyzed.

Typical negative inner dialogue contained in *What-now* baggage sounds like this:

- *My spouse is unhappy in our relationship.* **What now?**
- *We're going to have a baby.* **What now?**
- *I'm going to graduate from college and I haven't found a job.* **What now?**
- *I'm going to graduate from college with high debt.* **What now?**
- *I've just been downsized.* **What now?**

The key to dealing with this negative emotional baggage is to focus on opportunities and solutions. You can't move quickly if you are falling under the burden of your stress and concern, so you have to lighten the load.

List your *What-now* baggage here:

_____

_____

_____

_____

_____

_____

3. What-If *Baggage (Future)*

The third type of negative emotional baggage people commonly carry around is labeled *What-if*. It is usually packed with worries about the future, which result when people think about the potential problems ahead rather than the potential opportunities.

What if:

- *I lose my job?*
- *I become ill?*
- *The money runs out?*
- *The stock market crashes?*
- *I end up alone?*

There is nothing wrong with planning ahead. In fact, it would be wise to consider each of these *What-if* questions and come up with reasonable responses to each scenario. But there is a major difference between worrying about a problem and focusing on the solution to a concern. When we become fixated on problems, we become paralyzed. When we look ahead for solutions to a concern, we are taking responsibility and some measure of control over our lives.

List your *What-if* baggage here:

In this chapter I have asked you to invest a significant amount of your time and thought to begin to determine the root cause of your current attitude. So much was asked of you because it takes serious work to examine the roots of your current attitude—remember, you did not develop your current attitude overnight. Once we begin to identify the root cause of your current attitude we can also identify the triggers that cause a particular attitude to surface. For example, according to American psychologists, many people in our modern society have problems with rejection. As a result when many Americans are placed in a vulnerable situation, where they perceive that they may experience rejection, it triggers an internal reaction. This internal reaction usually results in the tendency to act out by avoiding the uncomfortable situation altogether or acting out the feeling of vulnerability by attempting to reject the other person first. An example of an external trigger is a person who listens to a favorite song and the song lifts their spirit. The favorite song the individual chooses to listen to triggers pleasant thoughts and feelings and therefore assists in the manifestation of a more pleasant attitude in the individual.

One of the most important steps you can take toward achieving your greatest potential in life is to learn to monitor your attitude and its impact on your life. You need to know what triggers a negative attitude and what triggers a positive attitude. You must then choose to adopt the belief that you can choose your attitude well in advance of any triggers. Monitoring your attitude allows you to know in advance what inhibits you and what motivates you. You can then choose to be what I call pre-active to situations! Being pre-active means determining in advance how you will *respond* to a situation you once would have *reacted* to.

I am reminded of a friend that had the tendency to react to situations rather than respond to them. This young man became hostile when he either had not acquired sufficient rest or had not eaten. He had little or no awareness of his attitude and behavior until an outsider brought them to his attention. After a thorough self-analysis over a period of weeks my friend discovered the reality of his hostile tendencies. He recognized that he was allowing external circumstances to dictate his behavior. With his new awareness he makes every attempt at getting sufficient rest and eating healthy. On the occasions when he does not succeed at getting sufficient rest and/or eating healthy, he goes out of his way to deliberately respond positively to people and daily challenges. With his superconscious awareness of his tendencies he has predetermined to respond positively. This is the essence of being pre-active!

STEP IV

"CHANGE YOUR BAD ATTITUDE FOR GOOD"

Attitudes are contagious.
Is your attitude worth catching?

—Unknown

THE HARD PART of learning the new is unlearning the old. A music instructor will tell you, it's easier to teach students a song they are not familiar with than it is to teach them a song with which they are familiar. The reason is students have the tendency to replicate that which they are familiar with and are less receptive to new instruction. In other words a student that has heard Britney Spears's arrangement of a song will try to sing the song as Britney Spears does. If the teacher's musical arrangement contradicts the Britney Spears musical arrangement, the student has difficulty unlearning Britney Spears's version and learning the instructor's version of the song.

Like the student mentioned above, you have gone through a process of releasing old thought patterns and behaviors that have contributed to your less-than-positive attitude. You will now learn ways in which you can change your once bad attitude for good.

Now that you have invested quality time and thought to uncover the roots of any negative attitudes, let us prescribe some antidotes to those negative attitudes. Two of the best antidotes to a negative attitude are gratitude and forgiveness. When we move beyond the hurt, anger, criticism, blame, and guilt, we are free to forgive, love, and count the thousands of things in our lives for which we should be grateful. An attitude of gratitude is guaranteed to improve your entire day—your entire life!

What others say or do no longer contributes to your having a negative attitude. Your own thoughts and the emotions you allow to live within you are fuel for the positive attitude you need to propel you forward. When you allow yourself to be grateful and forgiving, you'll be able to rid yourself of vindictiveness and judgment.

List the things you are grateful for:

_____

_____

_____

_____

_____

_____

_____

_____

_____

_____

_____

_____

_____

_____

_____

_____

_____

_____

_____

_____

_____

_____

_____

_____

_____

_____

_____

_____

A few years ago I rushed to judgment on two people who were working in my office, managing my bookings for speeches, travel arrangements, and financial affairs. The business was growing quickly, and they had become overwhelmed. One of them had health problems that added to the burden. Since I was traveling constantly, I did not see that they were overloaded, but I could detect that there were problems. I brought in some consultants to make recommendations. My staff wouldn't follow their directives. I felt they had the wrong attitudes. Realistically, they weren't equipped to handle the business because of its explosive growth. When things didn't work out, I decided to let an outside firm manage my business. They doubled the people in the office, but we experienced many of the same problems.

At that point I realized I'd been harsh in my judgment of my original staff that had been very loyal to me. I went to the two individuals and asked for their forgiveness. Forgiving each other allowed us to work together again. We became closer and developed mutual respect. We learned to appreciate our respective strengths and weaknesses. We reached a real sense of inner peace because there was no bitterness or hurt. We realized that we shared the same goals, and we created an environment in which we worked together to find ways to achieve goals.

It is important to appreciate and forgive people. Neither appreciation nor forgiveness requires you to maintain relationships with harmful and hurtful individuals. If you've been abused physically or emotionally, achieve a realistic appreciation for the lesson learned from the experience and sincerely forgive the individuals involved. Appreciation and forgiveness release you from the pain and anger. They allow you to release your baggage and replace it with a spirit of peace and self-empowerment.

Self-appreciation and self-forgiveness are important as well. I am amazed at how we sometimes believe it is easier to appreciate and forgive others than it is to forgive ourselves. We all need to realize we are not perfect and therefore should stop holding ourselves to unrealistic standards.

I have a friend who graduated from high school and immediately thereafter went to college. After attending college he began to discover he made a poor choice of schools. The college he selected simply did not suit him well. He became depressed. Soon after, he developed a rapidly increasing negative attitude. His negative attitude contributed to his doubting his ability to succeed as a student in college. His negative attitude influenced his behavior and he began to not study for exams, not do his homework assignments, and eventually stopped attending classes. Eventually, his behavior resulted in poor grades. He later convinced himself that his poor academic performance was proof of what he already believed—he was not college material. He dropped out of school.

After years of working odd jobs and living far below his potential, something happened that transformed his life. In his heart he felt that he was not living up to his potential. Being average was no longer acceptable; however, several years had now passed by. He was angry with himself, judged himself, and experienced deep guilt at having wasted the past several years of his life. By this time he felt he had disappointed his family and close friends and had blown whatever opportunity he'd had for receiving a scholarship for his college education. He was in debt to his former college and was therefore ineligible for any federal financial aid. He had a low grade-point average, which meant he was ineligible for any financial scholarships. He was broke because he neglected to save any money while working odd jobs over the past several years. He was in a bad situation. After months of wallowing in self-pity, my friend began the process of healing himself by forgiving himself for all the poor choices he had made over the past several years. From forgiveness came gratitude. He came to realize that, while he was currently in a bad situation, he was a citizen of the greatest nation in the world. He further realized that as a citizen of this great nation his possibilities were unlimited. He set out to find a way to go back to college in spite of his current situation.

My friend learned of a military program that would allow him to go to college full-time and the U.S. military would pay for his education. In return he served in the U.S. military, one weekend a month, as a reservist.

Though he later faced some personal challenges, he overcame each challenge with his positive attitude. To date my friend has succeeded in acquiring an associate arts degree, two bachelor's degrees, and a master's degree and is currently the president of his own small business.

It is important that we all learn to forgive ourselves and others. Here are some important points to remember when you are preparing to tap into the power of forgiveness.

- *There is no statute of limitations on forgiveness.*

  If there is a situation requiring forgiveness that occurred during your childhood, or years ago, it is still necessary to work through those negative feelings. Negativity allowed to fester will affect all aspects of your life. It is a cancer that will grow and spread unless you learn to forgive yourself and others.

- *Accept suspicion when you forgive others.*

  You can't expect the other person to understand immediately that you have made the leap from blame and anger to forgiveness. Approach the person in a nonthreatening way. Allow the person room to doubt, space to think, and time to see.

- *If you have missed your opportunity and the other person is gone, it's still necessary to forgive.*

  Try writing a letter to that person and one to yourself. Visualize yourself offering forgiveness to him or her. Tell them how they hurt you. Be very specific. Tell them you forgive them and you have released both your blame and your anger.

- *Don't deny, ignore, or try to overlook a hurtful memory.*

  Are there old hurts or grudges that you're still harboring from years ago? Or new hurts you're harboring now? Go back and uncover those areas and address them. Use the exercises in Step III of this workbook. If you don't, you will unconsciously carry an attitude that will reflect the hurt and anger you are holding in.

- *Understand that forgiveness may not be mutual.*

  When you're asking for forgiveness, remember that you can't control the other person's response. If the person won't forgive you, forgive yourself and move on.

Letting go of blame, hurt, and anger and replacing those negative emotions with an attitude of forgiveness and gratitude is a powerfully healing experience. It also returns responsibility for your life back to you. It's no longer anyone else's fault that you have not accomplished your dreams or achieved your goals. It's not anyone else's fault whether you are happy or sad. Once the blaming stops, you accept responsibility. I think that not wanting to accept responsibility is why so many people hide behind negative attitudes.

It may be true that someone else is responsible for something that happened to you, but once you've identified that something and that person, what purpose does it serve to continue blaming him or her? Let go of the blame, forgive and take back the responsibility for your life. Tell yourself that you have the power to heal through forgiveness and gratitude. Be accountable. Begin today to forgive those people in your life who have caused you anguish or pain.

An attitude of anger can be transformed into an attitude of gratitude and forgiveness by shifting your perspective. It is the power of self-forgiveness that allows you to forgive others. Identify the areas of your life where you need to forgive yourself. Write yourself a letter absolving yourself of the poor choices of the past. Commit yourself to making better choices in the future.

I FORGIVE MYSELF . . .

_____

_____

_____

_____

_____

_____

_____

_____

_____

_____

_____

_____

_____

_____

_____

_____

_____

_____

_____

_____

_____

_____

_____

_____

_____

_____

_____

_____

_____

_____

_____

An attitude of anger can be transformed into an attitude of gratitude and forgiveness by shifting your perspective. It is the power of self-appreciation that allows you to appreciate others. Identify the areas of your life where you need to appreciate yourself. Write yourself a letter absolving yourself of the poor choices of the past. Commit yourself to making better choices in the future.

I APPRECIATE MYSELF . . .

_____

_____

_____

_____

_____

_____

_____

_____

_____

_____

_____

_____

_____

_____

_____

_____

_____

_____

_____

_____

_____

_____

_____

_____

_____

_____

_____

_____

_____

_____

_____

_____

_____

_____

_____

_____

_____

_____

_____

_____

_____

_____

_____

_____

_____

_____

_____

_____

_____

_____

Now identify the areas of your life where you need to forgive others. Write a letter absolving those individuals who have hurt you, angered you, or otherwise offended you from their actions. It is not necessary that you give the letter to anyone. This is an exercise allowing you to release the past negative circumstances that have impacted your attitude.

I FORGIVE OTHERS . . .

_____

_____

_____

_____

_____

_____

_____

_____

_____

_____

_____

_____

_____

_____

_____

_____

_____

_____

_____

_____

_____

_____

An attitude of anger can be transformed into an attitude of gratitude and forgiveness by shifting your perspective. It is the power of self-appreciation that allows you to appreciate others. Identify the areas of your life where you need to appreciate others. Write others a letter absolving them of the poor choices of the past.

I APPRECIATE OTHERS . . .

_____

_____

_____

_____

_____

_____

_____

_____

_____

_____

_____

_____

_____

_____

_____

_____

_____

_____

_____

_____

_____

_____

_____

_____

_____

_____

_____

_____

_____

_____

_____

_____

_____

_____

_____

_____

_____

_____

_____

_____

_____

_____

_____

_____

_____

_____

THE
ATTITUDE
IS
EVERYTHING
WORKBOOK

STEP V

"TURN ATTITUDE INTO ACTION"

A positive mental attitude and definiteness of purpose is the starting point toward all worthwhile achievement.

—*Unknown*

OW THAT YOU have completed your "hard work" you can begin to identify a passion you have upon which you can begin to build your goals and your life. Often our passion is our most obvious yet most ignored talent: writing, music, athletics, singing, mechanics, cooking, and other natural gifts. What do you enjoy doing? What can you do for hours and hours and enjoy so much that you lose track of time? What are you better at than anyone you know? It doesn't have to be a great and unique talent, just something you're good at and something you enjoy. The level of your talent isn't nearly as important as the intensity of your passion.

When I lost the opportunity to play professional basketball, I thought I'd lost my purpose and passion. I spent several years wandering around with an attitude of disappointment. Looking back, I can see now that I came close to discovering my real passion once or twice during that time; however, it was several years later while working for IBM that I fully identified my true passion—public speaking.

In my first seven years at IBM, I was eager to please but I didn't have any direction for my career within the company. I was just hoping to find a comfortable and secure place, probably as a salesman, someday. At first, I was excited just to be at Big Blue. Basketball hadn't worked out. I obviously wasn't cut out to be an apprentice painter in Alaska.

Given my lack of other options, I felt fortunate to be granted a job by one of America's most admired and powerful companies.

It didn't take long for any attitude to change. It deteriorated into feelings of frustration and resentment. *Why didn't I get a better territory? Their sales numbers weren't any better than mine. I'll never get promoted.*

Some people join a company and begin swiftly climbing up the corporate ladder. My ladder ran out of rungs, and I joined the IBMalcontent club. I had a long list of excuses for my lack of success. IBM had risen to the top of the Fortune 500 because of its world-famous sales force. For thirty years, electric typewriters had been Big Blue's primary product, but that was twenty years before I came on the scene. High-tech mainframe computers were the company's bread and butter when I was hired. Yet I was posted to a low-tech office equipment division where I rarely made a sale, so I couldn't make my quota, which made me a noncandidate for promotion, according to IBM's policies.

I had done my best to fit into the company culture. I wore the right suits, shirts, and ties. I had the sales patter down pat. But my inner dialogue was self-defeating. *Maybe I'm in the wrong business. Maybe I'm just not cut out for sales.* In my mind, the source of my problems was always external. The negative inner dialogue was the result of a poor attitude, which itself was a symptom of a deeper problem.

It wasn't IBM. It wasn't my bosses. It wasn't my job or my co-workers. It was me. As I've noted in previous chapters, often a bad attitude is due to the emotional baggage we carry with us from one stage of life to the next. Sometimes, though, our negative attitudes aren't products of our past. They can also be an expression of our fear of the future.

When we feel trapped, bogged down, stuck in the mud, and going no place fast, we develop bad attitudes. Then we fall into the blame game. We find fault with everyone and everything around us. Once again, the enemy usually lies within.

Many times we get stuck because we don't know where we want to go in the first place. Think about the happiest people you know, the people with the most positive, energized attitudes in your school, on the team, in your office, in your family, and in your community. They may be from different walks of life, in different stages of their careers, but it's highly likely that they have two things in common. Those positively charged people are working on goals (purpose) while doing what they love (passion).

When I set my sights on getting a job with Big Blue, I did it with a very limited vision. I wanted security. I wanted the prestige of working for an internationally recognized corporation. I hadn't given up after not making the NBA. I had looked for new opportunities and worked hard to pursue them. But my vision was shortsighted. I'd set a goal with no passion or purpose behind it. I wanted to have a job at IBM—period. No wonder I became frustrated once I got inside the company door.

What happened to me at IBM is a case study of how a change in attitude can change your life.

I'd been a marketing representative in the IBM Product Center Store in Seattle for nearly three years when my regional manager told me that it was time I moved into another position. He was right. I was burned out. It was just a job to me. A safe, secure job, but hardly one I could get excited about. I was doing just well enough to hold on to the job and not badly enough to be fired, which isn't saying much, since at that point IBM still prided itself in retaining its people.

I was in a rut and had no idea of what else I was qualified to do within the company. My self-confidence was at an all-time low. Fortunately, there were a few people within the company who saw more in me than I saw in myself. Since I'd won a marketing excellence award for my sales presentation skills, my regional manager thought I might make a good training instructor for the company.

Training instructors conduct classes for new IBM employees, teaching them sales and marketing techniques as well as the basics of IBM products. I'd been through most of the training programs. I'd had some great instructors who could make the most mundane class interesting, and I'd had others whose classes were like watching paint dry. So I had a fair idea of what worked and didn't work for a trainer. A friend of mine, Ervin Smith, an instructor, thought I would be a good instructor too. He had recommended me to his boss, who talked with my regional manager and invited me to fill in for two weeks as a guest instructor in Atlanta.

My negative inner dialogue kicked in as soon as they told me about it. *Will I be able to master the technical material in such a short time? I won't be able to answer questions from all those smart trainees.* Comfort zones can be treacherous. I wasn't even *that* comfortable as a marketing rep. I just didn't want to leave the familiar for the unfamiliar, no matter how frustrated I was. It was not where I wanted to be, but I didn't see any particularly enticing options anywhere else.

I wasn't happy where I was, but I didn't know what I wanted to do. I was angry about standing still but afraid to move. A great many people are in the same situation. They hang onto dissatisfying, dead-end jobs because they are afraid to make a move. Here's a news flash for them: If you don't make a move, sooner or later, life makes a move on you.

That's exactly what happened to me. My regional manager took me to lunch one day to break it to me gently. "You aren't going anywhere as a marketing rep," he said. "You've got to go see if you can make it as a trainer in Atlanta. That's an order."

Once the boss kicked me out of the comfort zone and made it clear that I was going to Atlanta whether I like it or not, I woke up and changed my approach. I became Mr. Positive Attitude. "If I go down there, I won't let you down," I told him. "I will be the best. I will do the job better than anyone has ever done it."

By the time I got to the Atlanta training school, I was pumped up. I was determined that no one was going to nod off, complete a crossword puzzle, or write a doctoral thesis during my classes. I wanted their full attention, and I was going to earn it. It was show time, and I was the headliner. Strange things happen when you leave a comfort zone and turn your attitude into action.

Once I got up in front of those raw IBM recruits, I knew that I'd found my passion. There was one problem. IBM didn't need a trainer in Atlanta at that particular moment. When I told my bosses I'd found my purpose and passion, I ran right into a wall of bureaucratic brick. "There aren't any openings in that position right now, and besides, you know that IBM promotes people based on performance. Your sales numbers aren't that great. You aren't even the top salesperson in your store!"

I'd been ready to pack my bags for Georgia. Instead, the old bad attitude baggage was handed back to me. Even worse, a new manager was sent to our store. He suggested I might be put on probation if my sales numbers didn't get better. This new manager hadn't read my personnel file so he didn't know my stint as a trainer. He didn't know that I was dejected because I had found my purpose and passion only to run into a roadblock.

Before I could convince the boss that I wasn't a deadbeat, another bomb dropped. IBM sold its stores. It was getting out of the retail business. If I wanted to stay with the company, I had to go back to forty weeks of intense training in mainframe sales. Basically, they were asking me to start from scratch. If I didn't do well in my classes, I'd probably be tossed out the door.

I was discouraged as I began the training classes, but there was something about the training environment that stirred up the fire again. I was fascinated by the techniques of the instructors. Some were not all that good, but I learned a bit from each of them. Working in the retail stores was challenging, but being in the classroom lifted my spirits. It gave me a new focus and purpose—to become an IBM training instructor.

Have you heard the saying "When the student is ready the teacher will appear"? My new boss was a young guy, Craig Kairis, who had trained under me as a new IBM hire. We'd established a rapport and remained friends. His first words to me when he came to work as my boss were "This company doesn't recognize your talent. I'm going to help you show them!"

Throughout my career at IBM, I had a support team. Craig had been part of that team since his first years with the company. From the minute Craig became my manager, we sat down and mapped out a strategic plan to realize my goal of becoming a training instructor. He was in charge of a major IBM product announcement that all of the employees in the region were to attend. Craig arranged for me to be a presenter, to showcase my speaking skills. During my brief twenty-minute presentation, I raised the level of enthusiasm in the room. If you'd been standing outside the meeting room, you would have sworn there was a spiritual revival going on. I had those salespeople on their feet, shouting *Hallelujah!*

The one person who didn't make the meeting was the branch manager who'd been blocking my attempts to become an IBM sales school instructor. When he returned from vacation, there was an E-mail message from *his* boss wanting to know who Keith Harrell was and why he wasn't conducting every product introduction meeting and teaching others how to do it.

In the weeks that followed, I got call after call from managers around the region wanting me to do program events for them. Meanwhile, back in my sales territory, my numbers were up because Craig was giving me support like I'd never had before.

I had purpose. I had passion. I was on a roll. At the end of the year, my name came up for promotion, but the branch manager again stepped in my path. He insisted that I complete one year on a large account team in mainframe computer sales because he thought it would enhance my career. But Craig had been working behind the scenes, promoting my talents to the other members of the management team. When the branch manager balked at letting me go, the other managers outvoted him. The rest of the management team stood up for me. They saw that I had a purpose and a passion, and they bought into my vision. One important lesson I learned while in pursuit of my passion is that it was up to me to set goals for my life, and I had to direct my passion toward a purpose.

It is up to you to start making the changes today that will get you to where you want to be tomorrow. I once heard a speaker say, "In order to have the things tomorrow others won't have, you must be willing to do the things today others won't do." The fact that you are reading this workbook and participating in each of its exercises proves you are willing to do the things that only a small percentage of the population is willing to do. So go the extra-extra mile! Dare to dream, and set deadlines for realizing those dreams.

Understand that a goal is a determination of how you will get from your present experience to a future experience you desire. There are short-term goals, which are one- to six-month goals. There are midterm goals, which are seven- to twelve-month goals. And there are long-term goals, which are goals that will take one or more years to achieve.

Recognize that a course of action, better known as a plan, is required that will enable you to put your goals into action. Be aware that a good plan has two parts, strategies and tactics. An effective strategy includes a method of achieving a specific goal. And an effective tactic includes the appropriate implementation of the actual strategies.

Accept that there is no limit to where one goal can take you. Exercise the power of your attitude—your freedom to choose! Be creative. Imagine ways you can improve your life and turn your attitude into action.

List twenty-five things you currently desire to be, do, or have:

1. _____

2. _____

3. _____

4. _____

5. _____

6. _____

7. _____

8. _____

9. _____

10. _____

11. _____

12. _____

13. _____

14. _____

15. _____

16. _____

17. _____

18. _____

19. _____

20. _____

21. _____

22. _____

23. _____

24. _____

25. _____

Use the twenty-five desires you listed earlier to stimulate your thinking. Take this time to carefully consider your goals in each of the following categories. Don't limit your goals. The sky is the limit!

CAREER/PROFESSION (Meaningful work—Determining where your true career interests lie: changing vocation, advancing your career position . . .)

_____

_____

_____

_____

_____

_____

_____

_____

_____

_____

_____

_____

_____

_____

_____

_____

_____

_____

_____

_____

_____

FINANCIAL VITALITY (Getting out of debt, investing, saving for retirement or child's education . . .)

_____

_____

_____

_____

_____

_____

_____

_____

_____

_____

_____

_____

_____

_____

_____

_____

_____

_____

_____

_____

_____

SPIRITUAL (Praying/meditating regularly, reading the Bible more often, attending church, mass, or temple . . .)

_____

_____

_____

_____

_____

PHYSICAL/HEALTH (Eating more selectively, losing or gaining weight, starting an exercise program, improving your physical appearance, buying a new wardrobe . . .)

_____

_____

_____

_____

_____

_____

_____

_____

_____

_____

_____

_____

_____

_____

_____

_____

_____

_____

_____

_____

_____

MENTAL CLARITY (Learning a new language, learning new technology, learning a new set of skills . . .)

_____

_____

_____

_____

_____

_____

_____

_____

_____

_____

_____

_____

_____

_____

_____

_____

_____

_____

_____

_____

_____

FAMILY (Starting a family, improving communication and relationships within your existing family . . .)

_____

_____

_____

_____

FRIENDS (Meeting new people, developing closer relationships with existing friends, getting rid of some old acquaintances . . .)

_____

_____

_____

_____

_____

_____

_____

_____

_____

_____

_____

_____

_____

_____

_____

_____
_____
_____
_____
_____
_____

THINGS YOU WANT TO DO (Take a cruise, climb a mountain, write a book, start a business . . .)

_____
_____
_____
_____
_____
_____
_____
_____
_____
_____
_____

_____

_____

_____

_____

_____

_____

_____

_____

_____

_____

_____

THINGS YOU WANT TO BE (Giving, caring, sharing, understanding, thoughtful, intelligent, positive . . .)

_____

_____

_____

_____

_____

For each goal you identified, develop a long-term, midterm, or short-term plan (strategies and tactics) of accomplishment. Provide a calendar date for the day you will begin pursuing each goal and a calendar date for the expected date of accomplishment. Write down five important reasons why you chose each specific goal. The reasons will serve as motivation and/or inspiration when you and your goals are challenged with future obstacles.

My plan of action for _____ goal is:

_____

_____

_____

_____

_____

_____

_____

_____

My plan of action for _____ goal is:

_____

_____

_____

_____

_____

_____

_____

_____

_____

My plan of action for _____ goal is:

_____

_____

_____

_____

_____

_____

_____

_____

My plan of action for _____ goal is:

_____

_____

_____

_____

_____

_____

_____

_____

_____

My plan of action for _____ goal is:

_____

_____

_____

_____

_____

_____

_____

My plan of action for _____ goal is:

_____

_____

_____

_____

_____

_____

_____

_____

My plan of action for _____ goal is:

_____

_____

_____

_____

_____

_____

_____

_____

_____

My plan of action for _____ goal is:

_____

_____

_____

_____

_____

_____

_____

_____

My plan of action for _____ goal is:

_____

_____

_____

_____

_____

_____

_____

_____

_____

_____

My plan of action for _____ goal is:

_____

_____

_____

_____

_____

_____

_____

_____

_____

_____

My plan of action for _____ goal is:

_____

_____

_____

_____

_____

_____

_____

_____

My plan of action for _____ goal is:

_____

_____

_____

_____

_____

_____

_____

_____

_____

My plan of action for _____ goal is:

_____

_____

_____

_____

_____

_____

_____

_____

My plan of action for _____ goal is:

_____

_____

_____

_____

_____

_____

_____

_____

_____

_____

My plan of action for _____ goal is:

_____

_____

_____

_____

_____

_____

_____

_____

_____

My plan of action for _____ goal is:

_____

_____

_____

_____

_____

_____

_____

_____

_____

_____

My plan of action for _____ goal is:

_____

_____

_____

_____

_____

_____

_____

_____

_____

_____

My plan of action for _____ goal is:

_____

_____

_____

_____

_____

_____

_____

_____

My plan of action for _____ goal is:

_____

_____

_____

_____

_____

_____

_____

_____

_____

_____

My plan of action for _____ goal is:

_____

_____

_____

_____

_____

_____

_____

_____

_____

My plan of action for _____ goal is:

_____

_____

_____

_____

_____

_____

_____

_____

My plan of action for _____ goal is:

_____

_____

_____

_____

_____

_____

_____

_____

_____

Once you have completed everything outlined above—*put your attitude into action!* Don't fall into the trap of waiting for a "better time" to start achieving your goals. Do not wait! There will never be an ideal, perfect situation in which you can begin to achieve your goals. Do it now!

A word of caution: This does not mean acting haphazardly. Before you take any drastic measures analyze the situation carefully. Incorporate logic and reason, but avoid fear and doubt. There is a big difference! You may have to start out by making a minor change to your current situation until you prepare yourself to sustain a major change. Put your attitude into action but be smart and choose an appropriate action!

THE
ATTITUDE
IS
EVERYTHING
WORKBOOK

STEP VI

"BE PRE-ACTIVE"

The happiest people seem to be those who have no particular cause for being happy, except that they are so.

—*William Ralph Inge*

**VERY CHALLENGE SHOULD** be broken down to an opportunity. When you approach life fully aware that there are going to be challenges, you are that much closer to overcoming the challenge. Unexpected situations occur constantly. Our ability to maneuver through the benign as well as the traumatic challenges we encounter makes all the difference. That's why I believe being pre-active, being prepared to take positive action before a situation occurs, is so vitally important. Anticipating a situation before it arises allows you to plan a predetermined positive response.

I am reminded of a story that best illustrates this point. It had only been a few years after public schools were integrated that an African-American young man befriended a Caucasian classmate. They quickly became the best of friends. They spent a considerable amount of time together at school during their seventh-grade year. They shared many classes together including their favorite, physical education. Both of the young men loved sports, especially football and basketball. During physical education they always played on the same team and won virtually every sport event they participated in.

One day the physical education instructors arranged to have a major tag football game during class. For the first time ever, the two young men were selected to play on opposing teams. As the game began, these two "star" athletes played with intense passion in an attempt at helping their teams win. It was a very competitive and exciting game. When the final whistle blew, the team the

African-American young man played on prevailed—they won the game. His performance on the field was the talk of the day.

His Caucasian classmate became angered. He later said to his African-American classmate, "I cannot believe I let a nigger like you humiliate me like this." The African-American young man, not being pre-active, engaged in a fist-fight with his Caucasian classmate, over what he felt was a derogatory and unnecessary statement. As a result of their negative responses, both young men were taken to the principal's office and their parents were called, informed of the situation, and instructed to pick the young men up immediately. The African-American young man's mother arrived at the school first. She was a schoolteacher at another junior high school nearby. She often told her son if she ever had to take off from her job because he was not behaving properly in school, which was his job, he would regret it. Needless to say the young man was worried.

His mother met with the principal in private. After leaving the office she calmly walked with her son to the car. No words were spoken. On the way home she stopped by the market. When they entered the market she waited until she saw a vacant aisle and commanded to her son, "Go down that aisle and get some canned vegetables."

"Yes ma'am," he replied.

As he walked briskly down the vacant aisle, his mother, looking directly at him, began calling, "Jimmy, Jimmy!" She said it louder, *"Jimmy!"*

The young man looked up and down the aisle and saw no one. He turned and asked his mother, "Who are you calling? My name isn't Jimmy."

She responded, "Precisely! And your name isn't 'nigger' either. Therefore, I advise you to ignore any such reference in the future! That is not what or who you are!" In that brief instance the young man learned to ignore disparaging remarks and, in doing so, learned to be pre-active. Now an adult, he continues to approach life pre-actively.

It is important that you understand the importance of being pre-active, prepared, never giving up, never quitting, knowing you have the power to overcome your challenges. This is the mind-set you need to help you turn your attitude into action.

Several years ago, I was invited to be one of the closing speakers for a big IBM rally in San Francisco. There were more than eight hundred people there. I was still working for Big Blue at the time, and I considered it an honor to be invited to address my co-workers, including a group from my hometown, Seattle. I was excited. I wanted, and needed, to be fully prepared. For two and a half weeks I worked on my presentation. I practiced my voice inflections. I worked on my introduction, my main points, the body of my speech, my stories, and my close.

After all that preparation, I was fired up. I scarcely remember the trip from my house to the airport I was so excited. Once I'd parked the car at the airport garage, I ran to the ticket counter, only to be advised that the flight would be delayed four hours. Now, some may have taken that as a negative development. I looked at it as an opportunity to practice for four more hours, and I did, up and down the concourse. Out loud! As I practiced an older lady approached me and asked, "Sir, excuse me, but to whom are you talking?"

"I'm talking to myself. I'm getting ready for a motivational presentation," I responded.

She retorted, "Well what I've heard so far sounds really good." It was just the encouragement I needed.

Finally it came time to board the plane. I was seated next to a gentleman who for four and a half hours didn't say a word. He couldn't. I motivated him the whole way. When the plane landed, he jumped up from his seat and gave me a standing ovation. "I've never been on a plane with a motivational speaker, but boy you've got me fired up! You're going to do great!"

I thanked him and hurried off the plane, still fired up. My designated escort met me at the gate. She noticed my enthusiasm immediately and asked how my flight was. I responded, *"Anytime I get from point A to point B, it's always a pretty good flight."* She then went on to explain that she had some good news and some bad news. I asked her two questions, *"Am I speaking today? And is the audience breathing?"* She responded yes to both. So I told her, *"It all sounds like good news to me. I've been preparing for two weeks, and I'm ready to make a difference."*

To which she responded, "I like your attitude, but we have to move your speech from one-thirty to four-thirty. Also, you now have to follow Debbie Fields of Mrs. Fields Cookies, who is one of the top speakers on the circuit. None of the other speakers on the program wanted to follow her. We hope you don't mind."

Still I hung on to my positive attitude. *"Let me tell you something. It's been two weeks of preparation, followed by a four-and-a-half-hour flight. I'm so ready I'll follow anybody. And I hope she brought some cookies!"*

When we arrived at the ballroom where the conference was being held, Mrs. Fields was concluding her talk. My host asked if I wanted to go in to listen to her closing remarks. I declined, explaining, *"I would love to go in and listen to a great speaker like Mrs. Fields, but you have given me a challenge. And I've learned from my grandma that anytime you get a challenge you should break it down to an opportunity. I'm going to stay out in the hallway and practice my speech. I'll know when it's my time to come in."*

She said, "Good luck, break a leg."

I didn't know what that meant, but if it was anything good, I was going to break two. I started walking around the hotel lobby, talking to myself. *"Don't worry about Mrs. Fields. You know what you've got to do."*

All of a sudden, I heard the roar of the crowd. A voice came into my head: *"Oh, she's good."* Three minutes later I see two people leaving the ballroom. They're eating chocolate chip cookies. I said to myself, *"Oh no, you didn't bring them anything to eat."* Just then a friend came running up and offered these words of encouragement: "I saw your name on the program. Oh, Keith, you've got to follow Mrs. Fields? I'll be praying for you because I don't think you can be that good."

My attitude went from an all-time high to a basement-level low in a matter of seconds. My positive internal dialogue automatically switched over to negative. My inner voice said, *"Give up. They don't want to hear you speak. They want to go home. You didn't bring them any cookies. In life everyone fails, and today is your turn!"*

I believe there is a coach and a spirit that lives within you. When times get tough and you're faced with the hazards of life, call on your coach. In the middle of the hotel lobby, I yelled out, *"Be quiet! You didn't stay up two weeks and fly four and a half hours to come out here and fail. You'll make a lousy Mrs. Fields, but you can make the best Keith Harrell in the world. You're here to make a difference. Let's go get busy."*

I entered the back of the ballroom. I was all prepared to run down the center aisle. The top executive was introducing me, going through my bio. I was so keyed up I was jumping up and down. He kept going on and on with the introduction. My patience ran out. *"Hurry up!"* I yelled.

A woman seated to my right glared at me. "Oh, you're the next speaker. I feel sorry for you. You've got to follow Mrs. Fields and she was g-o-o-d!"

I looked down at her with a million-dollar smile and said, *"Let me tell you something. Don't feel sorry for me. The reason I'm following her is because she can't follow me. You better hang on to your seat and buckle up because I'm going to have an impact!"*

That situation turned out fine, but many times in life it's the hazards of negative comments from others and what we say to ourselves that contribute to our failures, destroying the support we need to stay focused and in control.

You must be clear on your goals and be vigilant about maintaining a positive attitude. When you approach life knowing there are going to be problems, you are able to understand that the problem is not the problem. The "problem" serves as a marker, or an indicator, that allows you to recognize where you are in relation to where you desire to be.

Learning to manage minor hazards is an important step to staying positive. One winter night, I was driving my grandma and my cousin Michael, who happens to be blind, home from Christmas dinner when I heard a thumping noise that sounded like a flat tire. This time I was 100 percent correct. I carefully pulled to the shoulder of the road and got out of the car. As I headed to the trunk, my grandma leaned her head out of the window. "Honey, if you need any help let me know. I've changed a few tires in my day, and I still remember how."

About this time Michael chimed in. "I can help you, man. Tonight I can see as well as you can out there."

I said to myself, *"What great attitudes. An eighty-six-year-young grandma and a blind cousin offering their assistance."* They were positive and willing to put their attitudes into action.

We're all faced with life's minor inconveniences and hazards. How much needless energy do you expend on inconsequential matters instead of facing up to the situation and continuing on your journey?

List twenty-five things you responded to negatively in the past week:

_____

_____

_____

_____

_____

_____

_____

_____

_____

_____

_____

_____

_____

_____

_____

_____

_____

_____

_____

_____

_____

_____

_____

Determine what would have been a more positive approach to the situations you listed above:

_____

_____

_____

_____

_____

_____

_____

_____

_____

_____

_____

_____

_____

_____

_____

_____

_____

_____

_____

_____

_____

Below, make a list of fifteen things that really push your buttons.

1. _____

2. _____

3. _____

4. _____

5. _____

6. _____

7. _____

8. _____

9. _____

10. _____

11. _____

12. _____

13. _____

14. _____

15. _____

How can you predetermine a response to those sensitive situations so that the next time they occur you can respond to them positively? This is the best way I know to steal the sting out of these situations. By exercising the power of being pre-active you render external situations powerless.

List fifteen pre-active responses to the situations you listed earlier:

1. _____

2. _____

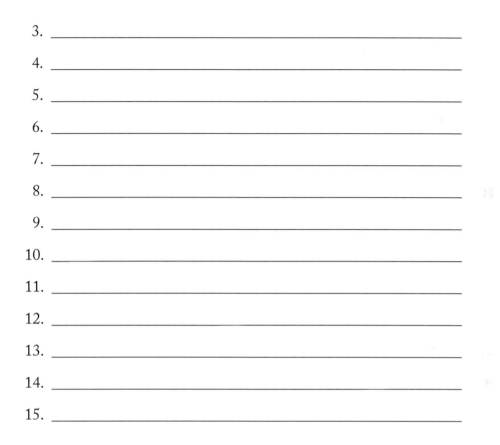

3. _____

4. _____

5. _____

6. _____

7. _____

8. _____

9. _____

10. _____

11. _____

12. _____

13. _____

14. _____

15. _____

When you put your attitude into action, you start to overcome the hazards of life. Once you accept that there are going to be hazards and challenges in life, you will be better prepared and able to adjust your attitude, do what you need to do to take an appropriate action, and experience the reward of victory on the other side.

As situations manifest themselves in your life make a mental note of each situation. Prepare yourself to deal with each situation in the future by predetermining from that point on the most appropriate, positive action you can take to turn each challenge into an opportunity. Be determined to get a positive result out of even the most negative situation. It is important to make a concerted effort to be pre-active in every aspect of your life—at work, at home, and in your relationships.

Life is never without the hazards of challenges, disappointments, setbacks, and problems. By developing a pre-active approach to life, you will become better prepared to face and overcome the hazards you encounter. Practice your positive attitude toward life. Deliberately establish the following attitude-enhancing habits:

- Smile, smile, smile, smile, smile! Make a conscious, deliberate effort to produce a winning smile at every opportunity. Stand in the mirror and practice smiling at yourself. Smile at your mate. Smile at your children. Smile as you walk down the street. Smile at work. Smile at dinner. Smile while watching TV. Smile while talking on the phone. Smile until your cheeks ache, then smile some more. Smile, smile, smile, smile, smile! Be excited about your life!

List fifty things that, when you think of them, see them, hear them, or experience them, make you smile:

1. _____

2. _____

3. _____

4. _____

5. _____

6. _____

7. _____

8. _____

9. _____

10. _____

11. _____

12. _____

13. _____

14. _____

15. _____

16. _____

17. _____

18. _____

19. _____

20. _____

21. _____

22. _____

23. _____

24. _____

25. _____

26. _____

27. _____

28. _____

29. _____

30. _____

31. _____

32. _____

33. _____

34. _____

35. _____

36. _____

37. _____

38. _____

39. _____

40. _____

41. _____

42. _____

43. _____

44. _____

45. _____

46. _____

47. _____

48. _____

49. _____

50. _____

Review this list frequently. Let it be a source of inspiration to smile, smile, smile, smile, and smile some more!

THE
ATTITUDE
IS
EVERYTHING
WORKBOOK

"DISCOVER HOW TO MOTIVATE YOURSELF"

*Have a purpose in life, and having it
throw into your work such strength of mind
and muscle as God has given you.*

—*Thomas Carlyle*

N THIS CHAPTER I am going to introduce you to tools that will serve to help you to motivate yourself and stay motivated. By the end of this chapter you will have acquired the tools that will equip you with the means by which you can begin to pursue even higher levels of personal and professional success.

Now that you have begun to develop an overall positive attitude, it is important that we monitor what we hear, see, and do. This involves making specific choices to monitor and minimize those negative influencers of your attitude. Avoid negative people as much as possible. Stop your internal voice, your self-critic, when it begins to send you negative messages. Replace those negative messages with positive and empowering messages. Be careful to avoid negativity in TV, radio, newspapers, signage, etc. Select to view healthy television. Listen to healthy radio or even better, listen to instructional/motivational audio material. Be selective of the newspaper and magazine articles you read. Avoid the negativity of the media to the best of your ability.

It is important that you become very particular about that which you choose to listen to, focus your attention on, and fill your mind with. We must be acutely aware of both internal and external stimuli that influence our thinking.

It is important to take a look at the nucleus of people in our lives that negatively impact our motivation to stay positive. Remember, while we have a choice in all this, our nucleus of nuclear (toxic) people can create an environment that makes it harder to stay positive. They come in a variety of different personalities;

however, we'll begin by focusing on four of the most negative, powerful, nuclear (toxic) personalities.

Personality 1 The Judgmental Critic   This type of personality tends to take it upon himself or herself to criticize your (and everyone else's) every move. They focus a lot of their attention on making moral value judgments about others. Their approach ranges from being openly critical and demoralizing to "Well, *I* wouldn't have done it *that* way." They even have a judgment about optimism—to them optimism is just another word for being naïve, unrealistic, and shallow. Their reasons for being judgmental and critical vary. Some people have developed a judgmental and critical view of life and others due to resentment. Others are judgmental and critical because they have a strong need to be in control of themselves and everyone else. Some people are judgmental and critical because they have very moralistic and opinionated views of the world and a very distinct set of expectations about how people *should* behave. Whatever the reason, the result is the same—they make us question and doubt our abilities and ourselves. And if we continue to listen to them, over time, we may find we believe them and then quit trying to be positive altogether!

Identify the *judgmental critics* in your life:

_____

_____

_____

_____

_____

Personality 2 Self-pitying Martyrs   These people are constantly feeling sorry for themselves. They feel that everyone in life has it better. They play the role of the martyrs, they complain about everything. They lack energy and enthusiasm and seem like they've already given up. It's OK for you to reach for the stars, but they'd rather wallow in the mud and not be bothered. They may even "suffer silently" while you expand your horizons. These people tend to have a dark cloud around them and assume that the dark cloud extends all over the world—except for the very lucky few who have just happened upon their good fortune. They have a real doomsday focus and a "why should anyone bother?" type of attitude.

If they feel protective of you, they may, in an effort to ensure you don't face the disappointments in life that they have, encourage you to:

- *Set your sights low*
- *Forget your dreams and expect very little out of life so that you won't be hurt in the long run*
- *Quit while you're ahead and "settle"*

These folks have a defeatist attitude and don't bother taking risks because "it won't work out well anyway." Their rainstorm follows them around and zaps the energy out of those who give it time and attention.

Identify the *self-pitying martyrs* in your life:

_____

_____

_____

Personality 3 Soap Opera Stars These are the people for whom life is one big soap opera. These people are often charming, charismatic, imaginative, compelling, and persuasive. These "soap opera stars" love drama and are often the star in the center of the limelight. Other people in their life tend to be supporting cast and cater to the whims and theatrics of their star. Soap opera stars can be very destructive friends to have. They tend to feed on the energies of those around them and create major drama, dilemmas, and problems in their own lives that they want your help in dealing with. "You must save them," and they spend your time and money getting them out of one situation just before they jump into another situation. To top it off, they devalue your reality. No matter how important the things are that you have on your agenda or how badly you need to spend time doing something outside of "their world," they violate your needs and charm their way into getting you to do something for them.

Identify the *soap opera stars* in your life:

_____

_____

_____

_____

_____

Personality 4 Bitterly Resentful These are the people who are bitterly toxic. They love to blame everyone else for everything that is going poorly in their lives. They're either outwardly or inwardly angry, belittling, resentful, and at times vindictive. Sometimes they will use negative, biting humor or sarcasm as a mask to say that which they do not have the nerve to say otherwise. Instead of using humor what they are using is "harmer," which is humor at the harm or expense of others. Their jealousy of others' good fortune and good works usually comes across with a set of excuses and illustrations of why they themselves are much more deserving. In their bitterness they have learned to be mistrustful and suspicious of others at every turn. In their minds their doubt of others' good intentions is often equated with what kept them safe in this world. Unfortunately, carried too far this mentality typically leads to isolation and weakened relationships.

Identify the *bitterly resentful* people in your life:

_____

_____

_____

_____

_____

While we may not be able to altogether stop the influence of the nuclear (toxic) people in our lives, we may be able to limit our exposure to them. First of all cut out the nuclear personalities that do not play a major role in your life. Second, minimize the time you spend with nuclear personalities that do play a major role in your life. Third, if the nuclear personality is a significant other, an adult child, a parent, a best friend, your boss, a co-worker, etc., be pre-active. Develop strategies to counter-balance the negative impact they have (Refer to Step VI of the workbook). Filter out the negative comments or actions of these major role players in your life.

In the interim, find people who are consistently positive and upbeat to play a major role in your life. Find others who take responsibility for their actions and are enthusiastic and encouraging to others. Give these people as much time as you can. Make it a point to call these people. Visit with these positive people. Create ways to spend time with these positive people. Appreciate the positive people in your life and positively support them. This act alone will limit your time with negative people because you will be frequently engaged in positive activities with positive people.

If you are thinking "I don't know any positive people!" then be a positive person and you will attract positive people into your life! I use the following activity as a fun learning opportunity to help others understand the impact of a positive attitude on others and themselves. Try this activity for one week and you will begin to notice a difference in your attitude and the attitude of others around you:

> While you are out and about working, shopping, at lunch, at dinner, or whatever, take these opportunities to be kind to absolute strangers. Approach such people as cashiers in stores or waiters and waitresses in restaurants and share your positive attitude with them. Share smiles and give compliments to these persons and others you may encounter. Observe the responses you receive from these persons. Observe the positive impact your positive attitude can have on others and yourself.

The above activity also acts as a stimulus to help you stay motivated. You will see that the more you share your positive attitude, the more positive responses you experience. Though you may come across a sour apple every now and then, the majority of the time you will meet individuals who are willing and able to reciprocate your kindness with more kindness.

The keys to self-motivation are affirmation, discovering your motives, visualization, attitude talk, positive greetings, enthusiasm, spiritual empowerment, humor, and physical exercise. I refer to these nine keys as your "attitude tool kit." By making good use of your attitude tool kit, you will be well equipped to seek higher degrees of personal and professional success.

Tool 1 Self-Coaching Through Affirmations Affirmations repeated several times each day, every day, serve to reprogram your subconscious with positive thinking. An affirmation is made up of words charged with power, conviction, and faith. Every time you speak, atoms of your body are affected; their rate of vibration is either raised or lowered. This process involves repetition, feeling, and imagining.

An affirmation is a method for affirming something positive in your mind. It may involve stating something that you think to be true even when all evidence appears to be to the contrary. An affirmation contains the elements of your belief, attitude, and motivation.

You send a positive response to your subconscious, which accepts whatever you tell it. When done properly, this triggers positive feelings that, in turn, drive action. Imagining is the process that allows you to see the affirmation in your mind. Once you can see it in your mind, you'll be closer to achieving it in your life.

Learning to craft a custom-made affirmation can be a powerful tool in helping you create a positive attitude and transform it into positive actions. The statements you design for your affirmations must be positive and in the present or future tense. An affirmation is something you say to take control of your thoughts, emotions, and attitudes. To work well, it should have these five attributes:

1. Be uniquely yours
2. Be uplifting
3. Deal with what is going on at that moment
4. Paint a picture in your mind
5. Touch your heart

Avoid using tenuous words such as *try*, *wish*, or *hope* in your affirmations. You want a statement that has the ring of an established truth, not a desire. "I am somebody!" has a lot more power than "I'm trying to be somebody!"

Some sample affirmations are:

- *Today I acknowledge my full potential and exercise my unique abilities.*
- *I will persist in spite of difficulties. I am unstoppable!*
- *I choose to ignore the critics and keep on moving in the direction of my goals.*
- *Nothing can conquer the power of my positive attitude. I remain focused on the positive.*
- *The three keys to winning are planning, preparation, and positive action; therefore, I plan purposefully, prepare prayerfully, and pursue my goals persistently.*

Over the next thirty-one days create a minimum of one affirmation a day. Your affirmations should vary in topic to reflect the categories identified in Step V. Repeat one affirmation a day, as often as you can, at times that are convenient for you. Feel free to create more than the minimum 31 affirmations.

1. _____

   _____

2. _____

   _____

3. _____

   _____

4. _____

   _____

5. _____

   _____

6. _____

   _____

7. _____

_____

8. _____

_____

9. _____

_____

10. _____

_____

11. _____

_____

12. _____

_____

13. _____

_____

14. _____

_____

15. _____

_____

16. _____

_____

17. _____

   _____

18. _____

   _____

19. _____

   _____

20. _____

   _____

21. _____

   _____

22. _____

   _____

23. _____

   _____

24. _____

   _____

25. _____

   _____

26. _____

   _____

27. _____

_____

28. _____

_____

29. _____

_____

30. _____

_____

31. _____

Tool 2 Self-motivation Through Discovering Your Motives   The first step in motivating yourself is to discover a motive that moves you. The dictionary defines *motive* as "that which incites a person to take action." Basic motives for action include love, self-preservation, anger, financial gain, and fear. The three strongest are love, fear, and financial gain.

You can learn to become your own master motivator by discovering your motives. What drives you? It is important to discover what motivates you in order to have the passion you need to achieve your success. Motivation is the hope that puts attitude into action in an attempt to fulfill a desire or achieve a specific result. Self-motivation requires at least five qualities:

1. *Enthusiasm.* To stay motivated, you've got to have goals that excite you and a plan that gives you instant feedback.
2. *A positive outlook.* Even when your circumstances may not be the best, you have to look on the positive side to stay motivated, because your subconscious mind accepts the information you give it.

3. *A positive physiology.* Changing your physiology can help change your attitude. Notice how different you feel when you smile, sit up straight, hold your head up high, or walk with a purpose. Try walking 25 percent faster and you'll begin to feel and look as if you have a purpose.

4. *Positive memories.* Good memories are money in the bank when it comes to shifting from a negative attitude to a positive one. When you're feeling down and out, you can always tap into a memory that reminds you how good life can be. I suggest that you help build up your positive memory bank by putting together a Win Book, where you put all of the positive notes, E-mails, and other things you receive from people. It's a book or journal where you can record the positive events and experiences in your life. Don't forget to write positive letters to other people so that they can build their own positive motivation based on your feedback. You'll find it improves your attitude, because what goes around comes around.

5. *A belief in yourself and your God-given potential.* This is why it is so important to take time to identify the talents, skills, and knowledge that make you a unique person with unlimited potential. When you know and believe in your uniqueness, you want to develop those talents and see them manifested.

Tool 3 The Power of Visualization   Phil Jackson, former coach of the Chicago Bulls and now with the Los Angeles Lakers, is a big believer in the power of visualization. In his book, *Sacred Hoops,* Jackson notes that he encourages his players to use visualization to calm themselves during time-outs in games. He advises them to think of a "safe spot" where they feel secure as a method for taking a "short mental vacation" before he gives them directions. Jackson said several of his players practice visualization before games, thinking about what's going to happen and how they will respond to it. Players say that pregame visualization exercises help them react more quickly in game situations.

Tiger Woods, one of the most talented professional golfers on the planet, says he uses visualization as well. Whether at practice or at play, prior to driving or putting a ball, he first visualizes where he wants the ball to go. Another visualization method Tiger uses is that of an instant recall of past successes. It's where doubt begins to creep in and in an effort to surmount the doubt, you remind yourself of your past successes. This, according to Tiger, requires mental toughness and assists in the development of one's confidence. Visualization is an important part of Tiger's winning psychology.

Nelson Mandela has written extensively on how visualization helped him maintain a positive attitude while imprisoned for twenty-seven years. "I thought continually of the day I would walk free. Over and over, I fantasized about what I would like to do," he wrote in his autobiography.

Viktor Frankl, an internationally renowned psychiatrist and author of *Man's Search for Meaning*, endured years of unspeakable horror in Nazi death camps. It was there that Dr. Frankl says he discovered that man's primary motivational force is his search for meaning. He notes how the power of visualization helped him and others triumph over the inhumane conditions they were forced to endure in the Nazi concentration camps. Many Jews survived their inhumane treatment because they were able to visualize happier past times and/or visualize a future brighter than their current situation.

Visualization works well with affirmations to improve your attitude and self-motivation. While stating your affirmations visualize what you are affirming. In your mind see what you are affirming as if it already exists.

Tool 4 Attitude Talk for Positive Internal Dialogue   Positive internal dialogue is what we refer to as "attitude talk." Attitude talk is a conscious way of overriding your past unconscious negative programming by erasing or replacing it with a conscious positive internal voice. Attitude talk differs from affirmations in that attitude talk can only be heard by you, while affirmations are positive statements spoken aloud with power and conviction.

We unconsciously say many things that negatively affect our attitude. Some of the most popular statements we make are "I'm sorry" or "You make me sick" or "I'm broke," when the truth of the matter is we are none of these things! The correct word choice in any of those situations would be "I apologize" or "You're disturbing me" or "I am experiencing a temporary lack of finances." You may say that it is just a matter of semantics and the words we choose make little difference in our lives. The words you choose affect your attitude and your attitude affects the whole of your life.

Write twenty negative internal dialogues you use frequently:

1. _____

2. _____

3. _____

4. _____

5. _____

6. _____

7. _____

8. _____

9. _____

10. _____

11. _____

12. _____

13. _____

14. _____

15. _____

16. _____

17. _____

18. _____

19. _____

20. _____

Replace the negative internal dialogues you listed above with positive internal dialogues:

1. _____

2. _____

3. _____

4. _____

5. _____

6. _____

7. _____

8. _____

9. _____

10. _____

11. _____

12. _____

13. _____

14. _____

15. _____

16. _____

17. _____

18. _____

19. _____

20. _____

Monitor your internal dialogue daily. When you catch yourself engaging in negative dialogue, stop yourself immediately and replace it with a positive dialogue. An example of this would be: James drives six miles to a gas station to fill his car up with fuel only to realize he forgot his wallet. James immediately calls himself stupid (negative dialogue). If James engaged his positive dialogue he would simply admit he made a mistake, learn from the mistake he made, and that would be the end of it.

Tool 5 The Power in a Positive Greeting Words have power. Most people greet each other with words that have the least power. Some average responses are "I'm OK" or "Just getting by" or some weak response along that line. By controlling what you say, using positive words with power and enthusiasm, you help to change your physical and mental state. The energy in your words gives you the power to impact your attitude and impact the attitudes of others. I advise you to use words that lift up your attitude and the attitude of others around you.

Instead of telling people how you feel, tell them how you want to feel. When I am asked, "How are you doing," my response is "Super fantastic!" Adopt a high-energy response to the question, "How are you doing?" Refuse to give an average response like "I'm doing OK" or "I'm barely making it." Be enthusiastic about your life, it's the only one you've got! Choose to make this life a super-fantastic life!

Also adopt a high-energy response to the question, "What's up?" or "What are you up to?" It disturbs me when I hear individuals respond by saying, "Nothing!" That's 80 percent of the problem—you should be doing something with your life! Refuse to give an average response like "Nothing" or "Just hanging." Adopt a knock-your-socks-off, high-energy response to the questions above or any questions like these. When someone asks you, "What are you up to?" tell them, "I'm working to make my good better, and my better my very best!" Be passionate about your life!

List seven powerful statements you can use to create a positive atmosphere when greeting others.

(An example is, "Hello. Isn't today a super-fantastic day?")

1. _____

2. _____

3. _____

4. _____

5. _____

6. _____

7. _____

List examples of seven sincere positive and empowering compliments you can pay to others to create a positive atmosphere.

(An example is, "Your smile brightens my day!")

1. _____

2. _____

3. _____

4. _____

5. _____

6. _____

7. _____

Below, list seven passionate and enthusiastic responses to enquiries from others.

1. _____

2. _____

3. _____

4. _____

5. _____

6. _____

7. _____

Tool 6 Enthusiasm, a Vital Tool for Staying Motivated   Enthusiasm is to attitude what breathing is to life. The English word *enthusiasm* is derived from the Greek *enthousiasmos,* which means "inspiration." The two root words are *enthous* and *entheos,* which means "Spirit within." Sincere and honest enthusiasm is an attractive characteristic that distinguishes your attitude from the average attitudes of others. You, mixed with half cup positive attitude and quarter cup enthusiasm, equal a winning recipe for success!

List five things that excite you:

1. _____

2. _____

3. _____

4. _____

5. _____

Tool 7 Connecting to Your Spiritual Empowerment   Many people find powerful and positive motivation in their faith. I happen to be one of them. I've referred to faith to make the point that human need is best met when fulfilled in the spiritual realm and manifested in the physical realm. Our spirit should act as our internal compass, leading us, guiding us, and directing us to our destiny. Whatever we materialize in the physical should have first been realized in the spirit. I reached this conclusion after carefully reading my *Basic Instructions Before Leaving Earth* (my Bible).

List three Bible verses that can serve as a source of inspiration for you.

1. _____

   _____

2. _____

   _____

3. _____

   _____

Tool 8 Lighten Up Your Life with Humor   Humor is a powerful motivator. Humor and laughter in your life contribute to more positive energy. Positive energy in your life contributes to a super-fantastic attitude!

There are also health benefits to lightening up. When you're able to laugh at life, your body muscles expand and contract, your blood circulation increases, and your digestive system improves. The body produces endorphins, which facilitate healing in the body. So if you want to live longer, lighten up!

Laughter is a perfume you cannot spray on others without getting a little on yourself.

List three jokes you can share with others that will make them laugh:

1. _____

_____

_____

2. _____

_____

_____

3. _____

_____

_____

Tool 9 Exercising Will Help Keep You Motivated   Physical exertion moves us from a low-arousal state to a state of high arousal, according to Dr. Daniel Goleman, author of *Emotional Intelligence.* To sustain your physical well-being, mental alertness, and physical and mental energy, exercise both your body and your mind. This is an effective way to experience a greater degree of accomplishment and confidence. Commit and discipline yourself to read self-development books, listen to self-development tapes, and exercise on a consistent basis. In no time at all you will begin to experience the powerful rewards of your new experience.

THE
ATTITUDE
IS
EVERYTHING
WORKBOOK

"BUILD YOUR A-TEAM"

As iron sharpens iron, so a man sharpens the countenance of his friend.

—*Proverbs 27:17*

FTER I'D GIVEN a speech to a business group, a well-dressed guy came up to me and introduced himself. He told me that he really enjoyed my presentation. He said he planned to use it in his business. I asked him what he did. He puffed out his chest and said, "I'm a self-made man."

"You are?" I responded.

"Yep!" he said proudly.

No one makes it alone. Siegfried has Roy, Ben has Jerry, and Barnes has Noble. No man, or woman, is an island. We all need people in our lives. We need their perspectives, their wisdom, their honesty, and their support. The strength of our relationships is one of the greatest measures of the quality of our lives. To a large degree, the attitudes we have about ourselves and about the world are the results of the feedback we get day in and day out from the people around us. To build a winning attitude, you've got to have strong relationships with people who share your trust and interests. I call my supporters my Attitude Team, or simply my A-Team.

Building your A-Team involves networking. Networking involves becoming affiliated with likeminded individuals and *working* toward establishing mutually beneficial relationships with them. Healthy and effective networking requires clarity of intent, compatible values, and a willingness to share resources and support to ensure mutually beneficial results. Your A-Team should consist of individuals who meet the aforementioned requirements and share visions and values similar to your own.

It's very important that you build your A-Team based on what you value and where you're going in life. In doing so you attract individuals of a similar purpose and passion as yourself. You will find it less difficult to build rapport with these persons. You will find it easy to foster an environment of respect with them and they will be able to do the same with you.

Being aware of your values gives direction to your behavior and justification to your actions. My values for building my A-Team are the following:

- *Integrity—living with high ethical standards*
- *Respect—treating all people with love and dignity*
- *Honesty—being truthful at all costs, being a doer of your word*
- *Accountability—recognizing the importance of personal responsibility*
- *Faith—having belief in your heart and hope and confidence in your spirit*
- *Love—having a foundation of support and unconditional love*
- *Health—being free of illness and physically fit*
- *Wisdom—having the ability to use your knowledge*
- *Compassion—having a loving spirit and a sincere desire to help others*
- *Achieving—accomplishing a feeling of success*
- *Recognition—being made to feel appreciated and important*

List your core values. Use your core values to build your A-Team:

_____

_____

_____

_____

_____

_____

_____

_____

_____

_____

_____

_____

_____

_____

_____

_____

_____

Often we are quick to evaluate what characteristics we desire to find in others; however, we rarely evaluate ourselves to ensure we possess similar, or at least complimentary characteristics. It's easy to identify the type of friend we desire, but are we that type of friend? It's easy to identify the type of people we desire to network with; however, are we the type of person those people would want to network with? It is essential that we evaluate ourselves as closely and as frequently as we evaluate others.

To initiate this process let us look at the behaviors that are essential to building lasting and supportive relationships and see how you fare. Use the following questions to stimulate your thinking to help you arrive at other questions you may need to ask yourself:

1. Do you accept others unconditionally?   *Yes* _____ *No* _____

Many people tend to have the attitude that friends, family members, and coworkers should always live up to their expectations, be available to them whenever, always be in tune with their needs, agree with them, and see everything from their perspective. When you set those demanding requirements for any of your relationships, you're bound to be disappointed. Engage in each relationship unconditionally. Accept that others will not always share your viewpoint or your agenda. They have their own perspectives, their own commitments to fulfill, and their own challenges with which to deal. If a person becomes involved in negative behaviors that are self-destructive or harmful to others, you should do what you can to help, but distance yourself if the relationship begins to have a negative impact on your own life.

Make a list of things you can begin to do that will help you accept others unconditionally:

_____

_____

_____

_____

_____

_____

_____

_____

_____

2. Do you earn trust by being trustworthy?   *Yes* _____ *No* _____

By offering unconditional kindness, honesty, and commitment to a relation-ship, you show yourself trustworthy and earn the trust of others. You can't expect people to honor you if you don't honor them. If you don't show up when you say you will, if you don't help when you said you would, then you can't expect to be trusted the next time. You earn trust one commitment at a time and then you keep earning it.

Make a list of things you can begin to do to earn a reputation of being trustworthy:

_____

_____

_____

_____

_____

_____

_____

_____

_____

_____

_____

_____

_____

_____

_____

_____

_____

_____

3. Do you do nice things without expecting
   anything in return?   *Yes* _____   *No* _____

Do you offer compliments to absolute strangers? Do you send unexpected, affordable gifts to friends and family? Do you write love notes to your mate? Have you done anything unique for your children? Random acts of kindness are wonderful gifts to others, but only if they come with no strings attached.

Make a list of nice things you can do for others without expecting anything in return:

_____

_____

_____

_____

_____

_____

_____

_____

_____

_____

_____

_____

_____

_____

4. *Are you loyal, even when it's not the popular thing to do?*   *Yes* _____   *No* _____

Loyalty involves honoring your friends when others belittle them. Loyalty means helping and encouraging others. Sometimes loyalty means telling them things they don't want to hear in order to motivate them to do more with their God-given abilities. True friends don't always tell you what you want to hear; they tell you what you need to hear. Goethe said, "Treat people as they are and they remain that way. Treat them as though they were what they can be and we help them become what they are capable of becoming."

Make a list of ways you can honor your friends:

_____

_____

_____

_____

_____

_____

_____

_____

_____

_____

_____

_____

_____

_____

_____

_____

_____

_____

5. *Do you listen to others to understand their*
   point of view?   Yes _____ No _____

Listening is a simple thing, but listening without judging is difficult. It is important to clear your mind and make sure the message being communicated is the message you receive. Too often we allow our values to enter the communication too soon and it causes us to begin to judge prematurely. We must first seek to listen, second seek to understand, and third seek to give insight or advice—but only when insight or advice is warranted.

Make a list of ways you can improve your listening skills and your ability to understand the point of view of others:

_____

_____

_____

_____

_____

_____

_____

_____

_____

_____

_____

_____

_____

_____

_____

_____

_____

Consider additional questions that will allow you to evaluate yourself. Look to the characteristics and values that you perceive to be essential to building lasting and supportive relationships.

1. _____

_____

2. _____

_____

3. _____

_____

4. _____

_____

5. _____

_____

6. _____

_____

7. _____

_____

8. _____

_____

Identify areas that require improvement and *work* to make the necessary improvements. Nobody makes it alone in this world. We all need supportive relationships to get through challenging times. In order to attract the people that are healthy for us, that share similar visions and values, and to begin to build long-term, mutually beneficial relationships with those persons, we must continuously evaluate ourselves and our relationships.

THE
ATTITUDE
IS
EVERYTHING
WORKBOOK

STEP IX

"DEVELOP A WHATEVER-IT-TAKES ATTITUDE"

Your goal should be out of reach but not out of sight.

—*Anita DeFrantz*

**FTER I MADE** the difficult decision to leave IBM to become a professional speaker, I had one final hurdle to clear. I had to tell my father. As I noted earlier, Dad spent his entire thirty-six-year teaching career at the same community college. He believed in job security, loyalty, and sticking with a job through thick and thin. He is not a guy who readily embraces or regularly seeks change in his life.

He knew I had mortgage and car payments that were considerable even for a single guy. He also knew that I had no speaking engagements lined up. No long-term clients. No guarantees. So I was not surprised that after I broke the news of my career change, he had a few questions and concerns.

"Son, it's not going to be easy. Do you have a contingency plan if this speaking thing doesn't work out? You've got a mortgage and car payments, and you don't have any clients. Let me ask you a few questions. Are you prepared to get a roommate?"

I responded, *"Whatever it takes, Dad."*

"Rent out your house and move into an apartment?"

I responded, *"Whatever it takes, Dad."*

"Get a second job?"

I responded, *"Whatever it takes, Dad."*

"Sell your car?"

"Whatever it takes, Dad."

"Move in with your mother?"

I responded, *"Dad, if I have to move back home, live in the basement, and sleep in the bunk bed, that's what I'll do. I am going to make it on my own because I know what I'm doing right now is what I'm supposed to do."*

I had towered over my father physically since the age of twelve, but I think this was the first time I'd ever stood up under his interrogation. He fell silent for a minute or two, appraising me, weighing my resolve. I was a student receiving one final evaluation. "Keith, you've convinced me. Son, you've got WIT."

I asked, *"What are you talking about, Dad?"*

"You've got a Whatever-It-Takes attitude—WIT. And that's what it's going to take for you to make it out there on your own."

With my dad's blessing, and a Whatever-It-Takes attitude, I launched a career that has been financially rewarding and spiritually fulfilling. The risks were well worth the rewards—believe me. Any time you want to stretch and grow, you are going to have to make changes and take risks. Change is part of life, and risk is part of the change process. To deal with risk and change, you have to adopt a Whatever-It-Takes attitude.

We make changes and take risks all our lives—driving on the freeway, starting a relationship, investing in the stock market, switching careers, moving to new jobs—it's part of living. If you're not making changes and taking risks in some aspect of your life, you are probably in a rut. Your attitude toward all aspects of your life probably reflects that rut. Bad attitudes can arise when we feel we aren't moving forward with our lives, often because we are resisting making a change or taking a necessary risk.

There are four basic ways to respond to life's challenges:

1. Shift into neutral

In this type of a response the individual develops an attitude of denial. When circumstances and events affect this type of person in ways he or she is not comfortable with, this person tries to pretend the challenge will go away or fix itself. Rather than being pre-active or responsive this person ignores or denies the situation. As a result the situation increases its impact and becomes a greater threat than it was initially.

If you identify yourself as one who responds to life's challenges in this way, list specific instances where you *shifted into neutral:*

2. *Adopt a negative attitude*

Negativity is the most common of all responses. The negative reactions to circumstances and events range from sarcasm to intense anger; however, the most common reaction is excessive complaining. Rather than focusing on a solution to a challenge this person continues to focus excessively on the challenge. No good results come out of his or her complaining. The challenge is usually accepted as being insurmountable to this individual and others around him or her. As a result the challenge increases its impact and becomes a greater threat than it was initially.

If you identify yourself as one who responds to life's challenges in this way, list specific instances when you *adopted a negative attitude:*

3. *Adopt a counterproductive attitude*

In this type of response the individual develops an attitude of defeat without making an attempt at surmounting the challenge. At the first sight of difficulty this person gives up or becomes destructive and begins to undermine any efforts to resolve the situation, contributing to the challenge rather than helping to overcome it. People of this type burn their bridges behind them. Their attitude is "If I am going to be affected by this challenge, I am going to ensure everyone is affected by it as well."

If you identify yourself as one who responds to life's challenges in this way, list specific instances where you *adopted a counterproductive attitude:*

_____

_____

_____

_____

_____

_____

_____

_____

_____

4. *Adopt a positive attitude*

This is the response that has the most benefits. It may not always be the initial response; however, this response can be adopted at any time and under any set of circumstances. In this type of a response individuals develop a Whatever-It-Takes attitude. This attitude is helpful to themselves and those around them. These individuals accept the challenge and set out to meet it with courage and confidence; however, their courage and confidence are not in the absence of fear. They feel the fear and move forward anyway, committed to doing (morally and ethically) whatever it takes to produce a favorable end result.

If you identify yourself as one who responds to life's challenges in this way, list specific instances where you *adopted a positive attitude:*

_____

_____

_____

_____

_____

_____

_____

_____

_____

Which response did you discover that most closely identifies how you deal
   with life's challenges?

_____

Is the approach you identified an effective approach for dealing with life's
   challenges?
   Yes _____ No _____

Which approach do you feel is the most effective approach to dealing with
   life's challenges?

_____

My friend told me that Murphy (life's challenges) has either just left your
house, is in your house, or is on his way to your house. That was his way of telling

me that we are never without challenge. While I agree, I have to add this point: If we are never without challenge, we should never be without a positive attitude with which to face these challenges.

Ultimately there are two types of challenges we face in life: expected and unexpected. Expected challenges are those you anticipate as the result of conscious choices you've made. An example of this may be a conscious decision you make to return to college. A reasonable challenge to anticipate would be that of managing the curriculum of your college courses. An unexpected and unreasonable challenge would be that of your college doubling its cost of tuition, making it unaffordable for you to attend. While the latter example is without a doubt a conquerable challenge, it can only be conquered with a Whatever-It-Takes attitude.

To assist you in developing a Whatever-It-Takes attitude, complete the following exercise:

Your doctor has informed you that you have one year to live. He advises you to review your goals and select the one goal you desire to achieve the most. He encourages you to relentlessly pursue the achievement of that one goal—what would that one goal be (refer to Step V if necessary)?

The one goal I desire to achieve the most and plan to relentlessly pursue is:

_____

_____

_____

_____

My specific plan (strategies and tactics) for achieving this
goal is (do your research):

_____

_____

_____

_____

_____

_____

_____

_____

_____

_____

_____

_____

_____

_____

_____

_____

_____

_____

_____

_____

_____

What are my compelling reasons for pursuing and achieving this goal?

_____

_____

_____

_____

_____

_____

_____

_____

_____

What is the specific date when I plan to have achieved my goal?

_____

My back-up plan for achieving this goal is:

_____

_____

_____

_____

_____

_____

_____

_____

_____

_____

_____

_____

_____

_____

_____

_____

_____

_____

_____

_____

_____

_____

_____

_____

_____

_____

_____

_____

_____

_____

_____

_____

_____

_____

You have one year from today to do "whatever it (morally and ethically) takes" to achieve the goal you've identified. Go after your goal with great tenacity!

A word of caution: Stay focused and keep your eye on the end result.

STEP X

"LEAVE A LASTING LEGACY"

*The opportunities you desire lie dormant
within you, waiting for you to give them life.
True opportunity is not to be found anywhere
else; not in your circumstances,
not by chance, not even by fate.*

—*Scott Holloway*

YOUR attitude is one of the first things people notice about you. It is also one of the things people remember the most about you. Whether you are a man or a woman of great accomplishment or average accomplishment, people will always remember the attitude with which you achieved your objectives.

In my book *Attitude Is Everything: 10 Life-Changing Steps to Turning Attitude into Action,* I tell the story of my friend Art Berg. Art Berg is one of the most inspirational people I know. The attitude he demonstrated while achieving every goal is exemplary.

Art was twenty-one years old, had just started his own tennis court construction company, and was about to marry his fiancée. He was living the American dream when a major, unexpected life challenge arrived at his doorstep.

One day, a friend went to sleep at the wheel with Art in the car. The car crashed into an embankment, and Art was thrown from the vehicle. His neck was broken, leaving him with little use of either his arms or his legs. His doctors said he'd probably never be able to work, have children, or compete in sports.

Art lost his business, and for a long time he was unable to get a job. He was advised to forget trying to lead a normal life and accept the limitations of his "handicap." But Art maintained his positive attitude about life. He eventually convinced Bell Atlantic to hire him. He told the company that if he didn't outsell their top producer in thirty days, he would leave without cashing a paycheck. He won three national awards for sales excellence in his three years with Bell Atlantic.

Art married his fiancée in 1985, and they moved to Utah, where he opened a chain of bookstores. In 1992 he was named regional Young Entrepreneur of the Year. In addition to everything else he accomplished without the benefit of his arms or legs, Art became a world-class wheelchair athlete. On July 10, 1993, he set a world record by becoming the first quadriplegic at his level of ability to race an ultramarathon of 325 miles between Salt Lake City and St. George, Utah.

In 1994, Art was featured in *Success Magazine* as one of the great comebacks of the year. Art founded Invictus Communications Inc. in Provo, Utah, to manage his growing public speaking career and authored two books, *Some Miracles Take Time* and *Finding Peace in Troubled Waters.*

In 2001, shortly after the world-class champion Baltimore Ravens defeated the New York Giants 34–7 in Super Bowl XXXV, Art was one of only two non-Raven associates to receive an authentic Baltimore Ravens Super Bowl Ring. Baltimore Ravens President Davis Modell presented the ring to Art for his contribution to the Baltimore Ravens by way of his inspiring life and motivational messages.

Such a devastating blow might have embittered someone else, but Art remained optimistic, enthusiastic, and giving. Art is a great example of someone whose powerful positive attitude sustained him and empowered him, even when he went through one of the most devastating tragedies imaginable. Art said, "Before the accident, I was looking for a way to make a living. Since the accident, I've been looking for a way to make a contribution."

Art Berg passed away Tuesday, February, 19, 2002—but not before realizing his goal of making a contribution to thousands of grateful people. Art's legacy of his unconquerable spirit and his love for life will live in us all for many generations to come. In the years to come we may forget Art's individual accomplishments, but we will never forget the spirit of his indomitable attitude.

Until this final chapter, learning to develop and maintain a positive attitude has been mostly an intellectual and emotional process for you. At this point, however, it is my hope that you will make it a way of life. Like my friend Art Berg, take what you have learned about the power of a positive attitude and dedicate yourself to living it and sharing it with others. Art's life story epitomizes each of the ten steps outlined in this workbook:

- *Understand the power of attitude*
- *Choose to take charge of your life*
- *A good attitude begins with self-awareness*
- *Change your bad attitude for good*
- *Turn attitude into action*
- *Be pre-active*
- *Discover how to motivate yourself*
- *Build your A-Team*
- *Develop a Whatever-It-Takes attitude*
- *Leave a legacy*

Don't think you have to have some extraordinary background or outstanding talent to make a difference. Who you are and what you can do is more than enough. Choose to manifest your power by maintaining a positive attitude no matter the challenge. Share your gifts, no matter what they are. Leave your legacy.

Too many of us look outside ourselves to determine what potential there is for our lives—to determine what our destiny will be. We latch onto the truth of other people's experiences rather than creating new truths for ourselves. We make their negative reality our negative reality. We make their opinion of circumstances our opinion, thereby making their limitations our limitations—their poor end results our poor end results.

We limit ourselves by race, gender, education, socioeconomic status, skills/abilities, geographic location, psychographics, and any other ascribed status we can attach. These descriptions of who we are supposed to be, that determine how we are supposed to behave, keep us inside the box. Think outside of the box. Live outside the box. Try new things. Challenge yourself. Be your own person. Start a new life. Live life on your terms. Art Berg did not care what it meant to be quadriplegic. He determined to live life on his terms and he did just that. You have that same power within you. It is stored in your *attitude*. Determine to live your life on your terms and leave a lasting legacy of personal power and positivity.

As a closing exercise determine what plan you can create for your life. What legacy do you desire to have?

The legacy of _____

\
\
\
\
\
\
\
\
\
\
\
\
\
\

In closing let us review the ten steps you've learned in this workbook. The steps are useful in empowering you to overcome the challenges of life such as you experience them.

SUMMARY

1. Understand the Power of Attitude

This key step is the foundation on which the other nine are built. It is imperative that you accept that each of us has the power to choose a positive attitude over a negative one. Our power is in our choice.

2. Choose to Take Charge of Your Life

It is important that you consistently accept responsibility for how you choose to respond to the circumstances and events in your life. No one else or nothing else is to blame.

3. A Good Attitude Begins with Self-awareness

One of the most important steps you can take toward achieving your greatest potential in life is to learn to monitor your attitude and its impact on your life. Recognizing the enemy (negativity), and understanding how it materializes, empowers you to replace the negative with the positive.

4. Change Your Bad Attitude for Good

By shifting your perspective you alter your life for good. Transform your attitude of hurt and anger into an attitude of forgiveness for yourself and others. Take control of your life by living life internally, on your terms.

5. Turn Attitude into Action

Start making the changes today that will get you where you want to be tomorrow.

6. Be Pre-Active

Make a conscious, deliberate effort to practice your positive attitude toward life. Meet each challenge, disappointment, setback, and problem with a predetermined positive attitude.

7. Discover How to Motivate Yourself

Make good use of your attitude kit. Use affirmations, visualization, attitude talk, positive greetings, positive responses to greetings, enthusiasm, spiritual empowerment, humor, and physical exercise to stay motivated. Do whatever it takes!

8. Build Your A-Team

Build long-term, mutually beneficial relationships—others whom you may share good and bad times with. These healthy relationships can serve as support for you when you are faced with challenging times. You can also be of support to those who have supported you.

9. Develop a Whatever-It-Takes Attitude

Do whatever it takes to respond to life's challenges positively. Create a unique combination of recommendations from this workbook that works best for you. *Work* to find the mix that produces the most beneficial end result for you.

10. Leave a Lasting Legacy

One of the greatest things we can do is get involved in something greater than ourselves. Plant positive seeds: seeds of hope, encouragement, faith, and love. Discover how you can leave a lasting legacy by making a mark that cannot be erased. Transcend yourself and reach out to make a difference in the lives of your family, friends, and community.

A FINAL WORD

Congratulations for successfully completing *The Attitude Is Everything Workbook*. The workbook consisted of ten parts, each part carefully designed to provide you with an opportunity to learn the ten steps for turning attitude into action. Furthermore, while reading the workbook you were given the opportunity to participate in numerous attitude-building exercises. Each of the exercises was designed to capitalize on the preceding exercise, gradually increasing in scope.

The goal of this workbook is to assist you in the development and maintenance of an attitude that works for you rather than against you. That goal cannot be accomplished long-term if you are to limit yourself to one reading of this workbook. A continuous review is required to get maximum results. Psychologists say it takes a minimum of twenty-one days to develop a new habit. If you are to concretely develop a healthy and positive attitude that works for you, you are going to have to work at it. I encourage you to go the extra mile and continue the process, as it is outlined in the workbook, for the next thirty days. Allow the steps outlined in this workbook to take root, grow, and begin to produce positive results in your life.

Each day, for the next thirty days, review a different section of the workbook until you have reviewed all ten sections a second and third time. By that time you and others around you will begin to notice a difference in your attitude. You will begin to notice a difference in the results you are getting out of your life. You will be well on your way to turning your attitude into action.

To assist you in managing your daily review of each section, I am providing you with a reading log. You can write which section of the workbook you read each day:

Day 1: _____   Day 11: _____   Day 21: _____

Day 2: _____   Day 12: _____   Day 22: _____

Day 3: _____   Day 13: _____   Day 23: _____

Day 4: _____   Day 14: _____   Day 24: _____

Day 5: _____   Day 15: _____   Day 25: _____

Day 6: _____   Day 16: _____   Day 26: _____

Day 7: _____   Day 17: _____   Day 27: _____

Day 8: _____   Day 18: _____   Day 28: _____

Day 9: _____   Day 19: _____   Day 29: _____

Day10: _____   Day 20: _____   Day 30: _____

PERSONAL NOTES

_____

_____

_____

_____

_____

_____

_____

_____

_____

_____

_____

_____

_____

_____

_____

_____